CREATIVE
ACRYLIC
TECHNIQUES

CREATIVE
ACRYLIC
TECHNIQUES

Practical Step-by-Step Projects

HarperCollins*Publishers*

Front cover painting by Susan Pontefract. Back cover
painting by Terry McKivragan. Paintings on pages 1
and 3 by Richard Smith.

First published in the UK in 1996 by
HarperCollins Publishers, London

Based on *The Art of Drawing and Painting*
© Eaglemoss Publications Ltd 1995

**A catalogue record for this book is available from the
British Library.**

ISBN 0 00 413306 4

Printed in Hong Kong

Contents

PART 1

Basics of Acrylic Painting

Exploring acrylic

With many of the advantages of oil and watercolour paints – and quite a few plus points all its own – acrylic is wonderfully versatile and a joy to handle.

Whatever your taste in painting, acrylic is well worth trying. Based on a synthetic, plastic resin, this flexible paint lends itself well to a whole range of techniques and is capable of producing everything from the most delicate washes and glazes to bold, thick, juicy layers.

It has increased in popularity steadily ever since it arrived on the art scene about 50 years ago. This is mainly because of its great advan-tages, particularly for beginners, over traditional forms of paint.

Acrylic is quick drying, has good covering power and great brilliance of colour – it doesn't fade in the sun as watercolours do, nor does it darken with time like oil colours. And, once dry, the paint takes the form of a flexible plastic coating which is almost indestructible.

You can use acrylic on a wide variety of surfaces. Paper, cardboard, card, canvas and wood are all suitable. It can also be applied on glass, metal or fabric, provided they are non-greasy and have enough 'tooth' to hold the paint.

Thinning the paint

In acrylic paint the pigments used are held together in a milky liquid plastic which turns

▼ **With many of the qualities of oil paints – but drying in a fraction of the time oil takes – acrylic gives you a golden opportunity to work quickly, laying on rich, thick, textured layers to convey intense drama, movement and atmosphere.**
'A port in the storm' by Gordana Bjelic-Rados, 16 x 26in

Tip

Experiment!

To get the very best from acrylic, try to explore and exploit its special qualities. Use it transparently if you wish but don't expect it to be exactly like watercolour; create thick, crunchy impastos and glowing glazes — but don't expect them to be like those you would achieve in oil. Experiment with different thinning mediums (gloss or matt), try out the extenders and retarders available from manufacturers, and also see what effects you can achieve with collage.

▼**Generous sweeps of the brush combined with a sensitive composition make the most of the limited but effective palette of colours chosen by the artist.**
'Knitting' by Sarah Cawkwell, 30 x 22in

clear when dry. Like watercolour, acrylic dissolves in water – you can use water to thin or extend the paint and to clean your brushes and palettes. But unlike other water-based paints it sets and becomes insoluble once dry.

On the plus side, this means a painting can't be damaged by water once it has dried. It also allows you to overpaint and correct mistakes. The disadvantage is that acrylic can damage your brushes and palettes. If the paint is left to dry on brushes they become almost impossible to clean. You need to rinse them regularly and never let paint dry on them.

Water isn't the only medium used to thin or extend acrylic. Most acrylic paint manufacturers produce their own painting mediums which change the way acrylic behaves. The two most important are gloss and matt. Gloss medium thins acrylic paint so that it flows easily and dries to a shiny finish like an oil painting. Matt medium has exactly the same consistency but dries to a non-shiny finish.

Cutting down on drying time

The outstanding quality of acrylic paint is the speed at which it dries. It becomes touch-dry as soon as the water content evaporates and can usually be overpainted within 30 minutes. This is marvellous if you need to work quickly – to capture the fleeting effects of light on a landscape, for example.

You can also lay in an underpainting and overpaint with layers almost at once without the long drying times required for oil. And at the end of a day painting outdoors you have a dry paper or canvas to take home rather than an oily surface which is difficult to carry and always seems to fall butter-side-down. Even thick layers of paint have a touch-dry surface at the end of the day.

Acrylic underpainting

Once acrylic is dry it can be used as a base for other media. You can combine acrylic and oil very effectively, laying in the underpainting in fast-drying acrylic then completing the painting in oil using traditional oil techniques. This approach allows you to block in the broad structures of the composition and cover the white of the canvas very quickly, but then develop the painting in a more considered way in oil. (Remember that you can use oil paints over acrylic – but never try to put acrylic paints over oil.)

A combination of acrylic and oil is a useful way of working outdoors – using acrylic paint in the field but completing the painting in oil in the studio. This approach is similar to that used by the Flemish Old Masters who laid in

▲ **Simple brushstrokes in the vibrant colours that are the hallmark of acrylic paints combine in this pleasing scene.**
'Vailhourles 1' by Terry Burke, coloured paper, 52 x 38cm

► Versatile brushwork,
with many bold strokes and
lines, gives masses of interesting texture in this painting.
'Busk' by Bill Taylor, acrylic on
card/cardboard, 13 x10in

▼ Though lending itself well
to covering large areas of
canvas or paper, acrylic is also
capable of great delicacy and
precision. Here the artist has
achieved a wide variety of
different textures and also a
high degree of realism.
'Waiting for mum' by Richard J Smith,
acrylic on board, 32 x 24in

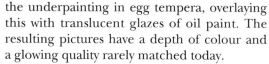

the underpainting in egg tempera, overlaying
this with translucent glazes of oil paint. The
resulting pictures have a depth of colour and
a glowing quality rarely matched today.

You can also combine acrylic paints with
many other media – oil pastel, pastel, crayon
and pencil are just some of the possibilities.

As well as being fast drying and unaffected
by water once dry, acrylic is highly adhesive.
This makes it excellent for outdoor murals – it
is weather resistant and adheres well to most
surfaces. It is also good for collage techniques
since the undiluted paint and the various
mediums can be used to glue paper or fabrics
to the support.

Acrylic texture pastes (gels) and modelling
mediums are especially strong adhesives and
can also be used to create relief surfaces.

A range of approaches

Thinned with water and used on paper,
acrylic can be used to create transparent
washes which closely resemble watercolour or
gouache. Using it directly from the tube or
very slightly thinned, you can build up rich
impastos – as with oil. It is equally good for
small-scale works on paper and for large easel
paintings on canvas.

Not all acrylic paints are the same – some
are more fluid than others. Some makers give
only one formula while others offer the paint
in a buttery consistency, rather like oil paint,
and in a more fluid form as well. The thicker
paints are better for impasto techniques
where the mark of the brush is important,
while flow formula is excellent for large-scale
staining techniques.

Choosing acrylic paints

Today the range of acrylic paints is simply vast. With information about the most recent developments, you can use the right paint for the right job, saving yourself time, money and a lot of hard work.

Paint manufacturers are constantly developing and changing their acrylic paints. This is tremendously exciting – but keeping informed about current products is not easy. Even experienced professionals may miss out on new possibilities because they are unfamiliar with recent developments.

Liquid acrylics are a typical example. Fairly new products, they slightly resemble brilliant liquid watercolours or inks (which tend to be fugitive – fading when exposed to light). Because they all look similar they may often be grouped together – wrongly, since most liquid acrylics are permanent, not fugitive. If artists don't know about them, they're limiting their creative possibilities.

What is acrylic?

Acrylic paint is simply pigment dispersed in a film of transparent liquid plastic (technically speaking, an emulsion consisting of plastic acrylic resin and water). You can dilute acrylic paint with water, but remember that it is completely insoluble once dry.

In its liquid form the emulsion has a milky appearance, but after the water evaporates it is transparent. You can test this with one of the acrylic mediums – just brush some undiluted gloss or matt medium (an emulsion without any pigment) on to a tinted support. You'll see that it's rich and creamy straight out of the bottle, but completely transparent when dry.

Types of paint

Most paint manufacturers have at least one range of acrylic paint in their catalogue – and some have several. The main differences between one range and another are the consistency and the number of colours.

You can apply acrylics thickly for impasto and thinly for washes and staining techniques. Thick, textured impasto requires a stiff paint which can retain the strong mark of the brush or painting knife. Thinner, more fluid paint is best for washes. Adding proprietary mediums to thicken or thin the paint is one way to increase the paint's versatility.

Some manufacturers, however, produce several ranges of paint with different consistencies to save you the time and trouble of mixing. Here we look at three of the largest acrylic paint manufacturers. Their products are widely available in most art shops.

DID YOU KNOW?

What are alkyds?
Often confused with acrylics, alkyds are fast-drying oil paints (but not as fast as acrylic paints) that do not mix with water. Use them on their own, or combine them with oil paints. To modify the way alkyds behave and to quicken their drying time, use alkyd mediums such as Winsor & Newton's Wingel or Liquin.

▼ **Here the artist's use of opaque acrylic is bold and loose. The scumbled water and the sky give a dramatic sense of depth, helping your eye to travel from the opaque water to the bright red building and into the city-scape and beyond.**
'St Paul's from the South Bank' by Terry McKivragan, acrylic on hardboard, 36 ¼ x 44in

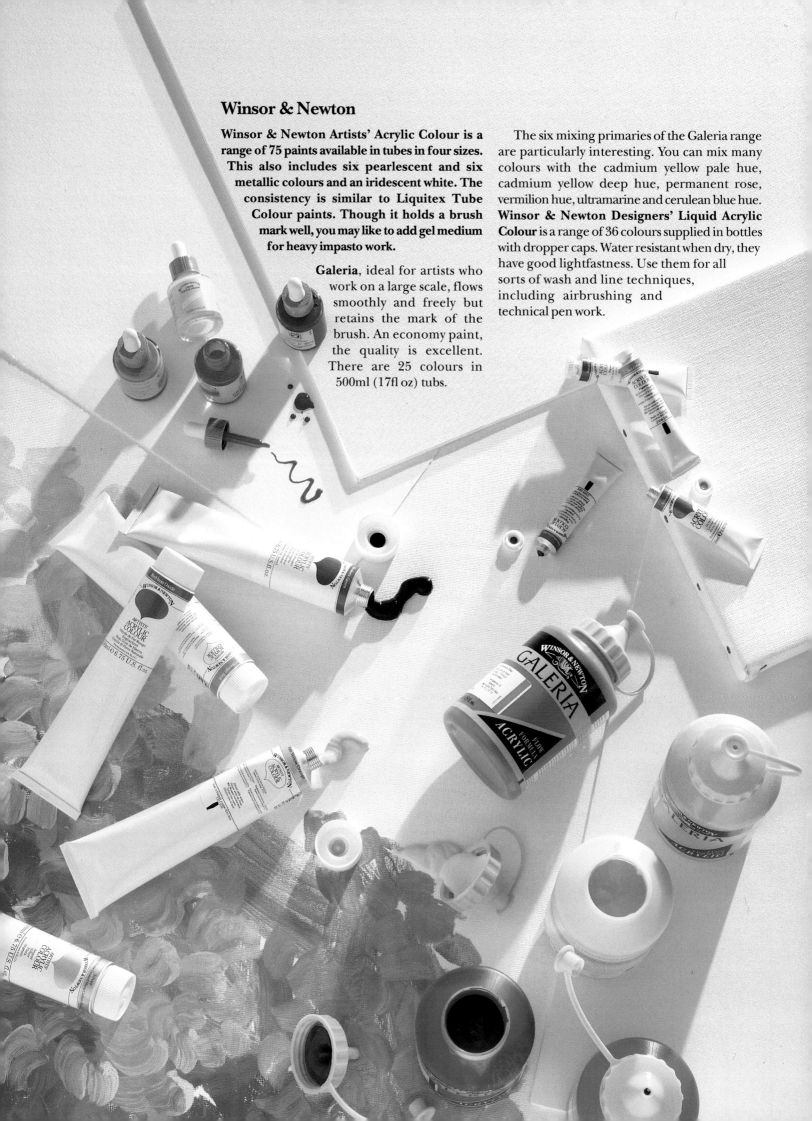

Winsor & Newton

Winsor & Newton Artists' Acrylic Colour is a range of 75 paints available in tubes in four sizes. This also includes six pearlescent and six metallic colours and an iridescent white. The consistency is similar to Liquitex Tube Colour paints. Though it holds a brush mark well, you may like to add gel medium for heavy impasto work.

Galeria, ideal for artists who work on a large scale, flows smoothly and freely but retains the mark of the brush. An economy paint, the quality is excellent. There are 25 colours in 500ml (17fl oz) tubs.

The six mixing primaries of the Galeria range are particularly interesting. You can mix many colours with the cadmium yellow pale hue, cadmium yellow deep hue, permanent rose, vermilion hue, ultramarine and cerulean blue hue. **Winsor & Newton Designers' Liquid Acrylic Colour** is a range of 36 colours supplied in bottles with dropper caps. Water resistant when dry, they have good lightfastness. Use them for all sorts of wash and line techniques, including airbrushing and technical pen work.

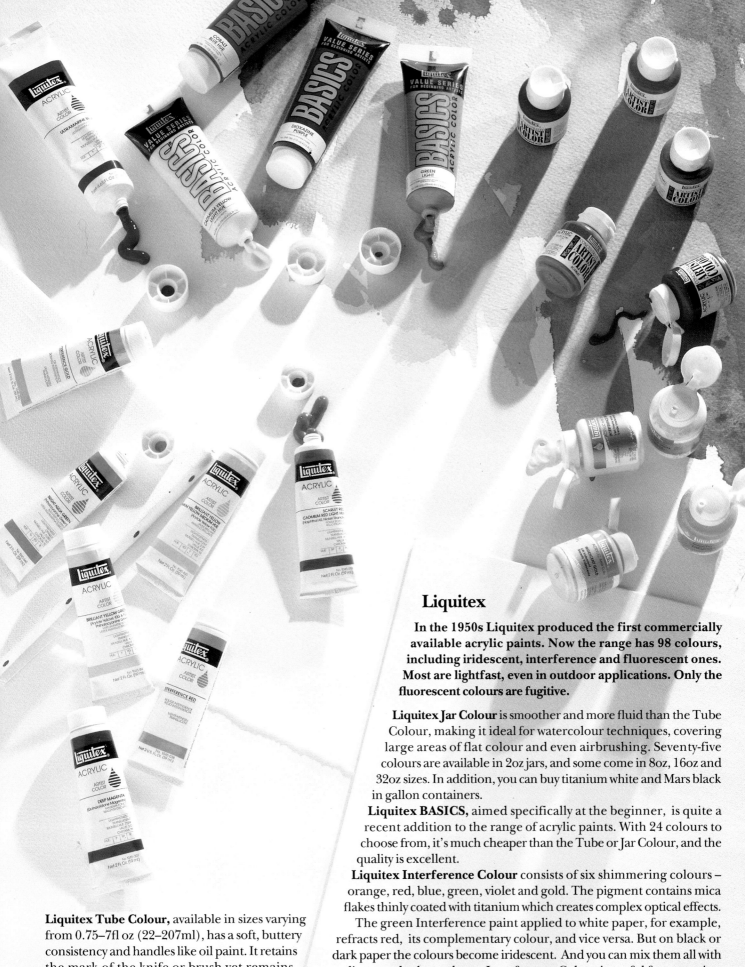

Liquitex

In the 1950s Liquitex produced the first commercially available acrylic paints. Now the range has 98 colours, including iridescent, interference and fluorescent ones. Most are lightfast, even in outdoor applications. Only the fluorescent colours are fugitive.

Liquitex Jar Colour is smoother and more fluid than the Tube Colour, making it ideal for watercolour techniques, covering large areas of flat colour and even airbrushing. Seventy-five colours are available in 2oz jars, and some come in 8oz, 16oz and 32oz sizes. In addition, you can buy titanium white and Mars black in gallon containers.

Liquitex BASICS, aimed specifically at the beginner, is quite a recent addition to the range of acrylic paints. With 24 colours to choose from, it's much cheaper than the Tube or Jar Colour, and the quality is excellent.

Liquitex Interference Colour consists of six shimmering colours – orange, red, blue, green, violet and gold. The pigment contains mica flakes thinly coated with titanium which creates complex optical effects. The green Interference paint applied to white paper, for example, refracts red, its complementary colour, and vice versa. But on black or dark paper the colours become iridescent. And you can mix them all with mediums and other colours. Interference Colour is useful for capturing the iridescent qualities on some bird plumages, for instance.

Liquitex Fluorescent Colour appears to glow even when mixed with other acrylic paints. Don't use it for paintings you want to keep because it's fugitive.

Liquitex Tube Colour, available in sizes varying from 0.75–7fl oz (22–207ml), has a soft, buttery consistency and handles like oil paint. It retains the mark of the knife or brush yet remains flexible when dry. The complete range isn't available in all tube sizes. Mars and ivory black come in large 8fl oz (237ml) tubes.

Daler-Rowney

Daler-Rowney offers a range of 55 colours in two consistencies – Cryla and Cryla Flow.

Cryla has a creamy consistency and is good for impasto work. There are 38ml and 120ml tubes and a limited selection of colours in 2.2 litre tubs.

Cryla Flow is thinner and more suitable for washes, staining techniques and large-scale work. It's available in 60ml tubes, plus a 120ml tube of white. Some colours come in 2.2 litre tubs.

Rowney System 3 Acrylic is a range of 24 colours in 500ml nozzle-cap pots. A quality product at an economical price, it is compatible with Daler-Rowney acrylic mediums and is ideal for school and craft work and for large-scale projects such as murals.

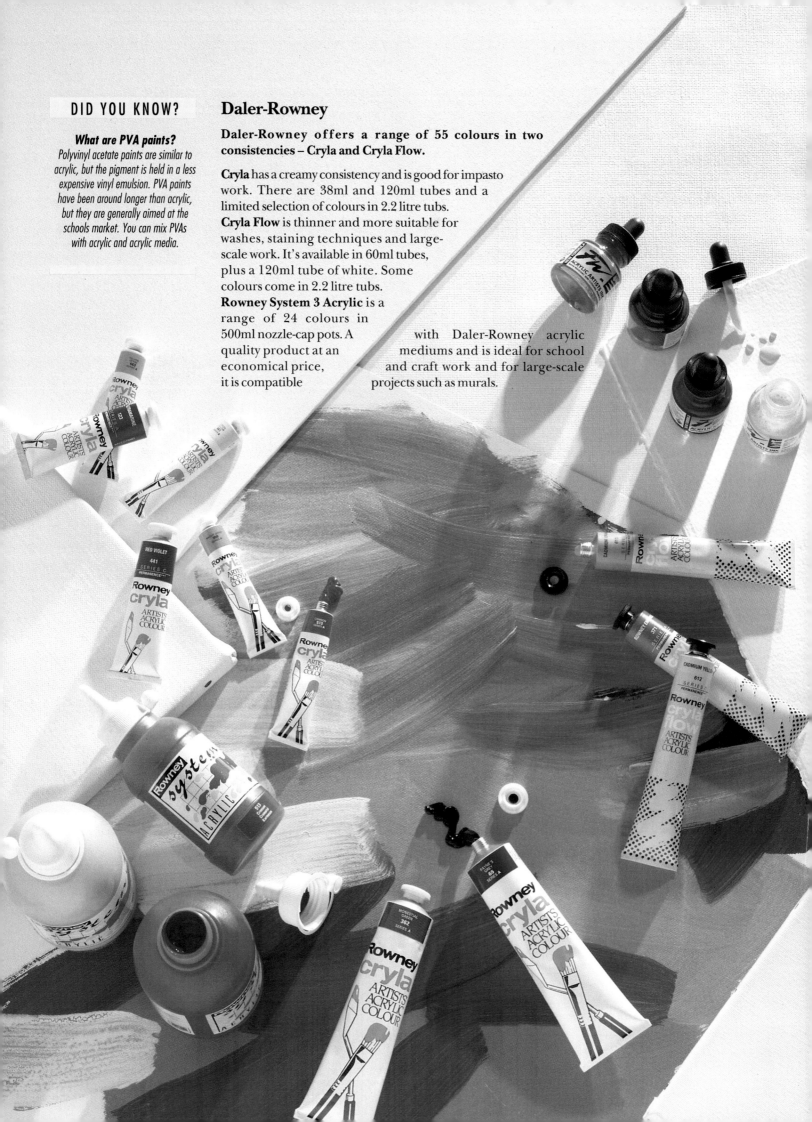

Liquid acrylics

Liquid acrylics – the most fluid form of acrylic paint – come in many dazzling transparent and opaque colours.

Acrylic paints exist in many forms – from buttery, paste-like consistencies through to liquids. Because they're fairly new (40 or so years old compared with 500 years for oils), manufacturers haven't standardized the range of products, and this causes a lot of confusion for artists – beginners and experienced alike. Liquid acrylics are a typical example – they're so fluid that they closely resemble traditional coloured inks and brilliant liquid watercolours.

Traditional coloured inks are bound with shellac (an alcohol-soluble resin made from insect secretions). They are waterproof when dry and tend to be made from dyes. Generally, they are not lightfast, but some colours, such as black and white, are more lightfast than others.

Brilliant liquid watercolours are bound with gum arabic. Like the inks, they are not generally lightfast but are water soluble when dry.

Liquid acrylics are bound with a film of transparent liquid plastic (acrylic). They are water resistant when dry and tend to be more transparent and flexible than shellac-based inks. Their advantage is that they are made from pigments, which are generally more lightfast than dyes.

Lightfastness

Why would anyone want to use a fugitive dye or a pigment, no matter how beautiful the effect? The reason is that coloured inks and brilliant watercolours were originally designed for graphic illustrations which are turned into printed matter such as greeting cards,

Royal Sovereign's Magic Colour Liquid Acrylics

▲ **Liquid acrylics can be used in the same way as watercolour or ink. They have similar depth of colour to inks, but they are generally more lightfast.**
'Caught between day and night' by Jennifer Tuffs, Magic Colour Liquid Acrylics on watercolour paper, 9 x 12in

DID YOU KNOW?

Popular medium
Acrylics were first developed for industrial use in the 1920s. It wasn't until the1950s and '60s that they really came to the attention of artists, when they were used by American Pop Art painters for their brightly coloured images of the modern world — of soup cans, billboards and cartoon characters. Later, David Hockney did much to establish their popularity in Europe.

Rotring's ACP Liquid Acrylics

books or posters. So it doesn't matter if the original artwork has a limited life because the printed version will be lightfast. However, the artworks can be stored away from the light to prevent some fading.

But no matter how seductive the colours and brilliance of dye-based inks and concentrated liquid watercolours, don't use them for fine artworks which you intend to keep for a long time – inevitably they will fade rapidly.

Lascaux's Aquacryl

Royal Sovereign's Magic Colours

Using liquid acrylics

These paints are densely pigmented – in other words, a little goes a long way. You can mix all the colours to create an endless range of transparent colours, or add a little white to create opaque paint.

Supports Your choice of support with liquid acrylics is vast – cardboard, watercolour paper, millboard, canvas board and even sheets of acetate. And you can create vibrant stained effects on raw canvas, either to produce a finished image or to use as an underpainting.

Drawing Liquid acrylics even work well in technical pens for precise, detailed drawing such as in architectural studies. They are also a boon for calligraphy, allowing you to create beautiful flowing lines with dip and reservoir pens. Because liquid acrylics are water resistant when dry, you must *always* wash the dip pens in water after use, and replace the cap firmly on reservoir and technical pens. Flush reservoir pens thoroughly with water after use to prevent paint from drying up inside. If the paint does dry inside, clean it out with airbrush cleaning fluid.

Watercolours You can use liquid acrylics with a soft brush for traditional watercolour techniques such as wet-in-wet and wet-on-dry. Also try mixing the colours together by pouring, dripping and tipping to create wonderful rainbow effects. Try

▶ **Use the dropper caps on some bottles of liquid acrylics to transfer paint to a watercolour palette or to drop paint straight on to your painting. If you use a dropper cap, there is no fear of contaminating the colour in the bottle with another paint colour.**

using a straw to blow rivers of colour across the support, or use a hair dryer to create even more dramatic results.

Crafts Liquid acrylics have many craft applications – they are excellent for decorating resin, wood and leather. You can create stained-glass effects by applying them to glass. (In some cases manufacturers recommend a medium to improve adhesion to smooth surfaces.)

Mixed media It's also possible to combine other media successfully with liquid acrylics – for example, watercolours, gouache, other acrylics, pastel and pencil. You can achieve stunning effects by applying transparent colours over pearlescent acrylics, such as Daler-Rowney's Pearlescent Liquid Acrylics, or Liquitex's concentrated Opalescent Acrylic Colour.

Winsor & Newton's Designers' Liquid Acrylics

Daler-Rowney's FW Acrylic Artists' Inks

Decorative paper on cardboard

▶**1** Our artist wanted to use this paper's pattern as the background for her next leaf painting. Although the paper is quite strong and unlikely to tear, she thought it was better to mount it on cardboard or thin card to stop it from curling over when wet.

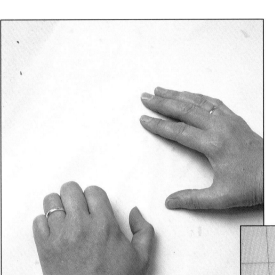

▲**2** Brush diluted Liquitex matte gel medium on to the back of the paper with the decorator's brush. Brush it out well to leave a thin, even layer. Place the paper on the card carefully and smooth away any air bubbles, working from the middle of the sheet to the edges. Do this through a sheet of spare paper to avoid getting grease or dirt marks on the surface. For more pressure, smooth the paper with the back of a spoon or a rubber roller.

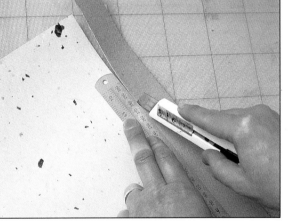

◀**3** The sheet of paper was smaller than the supporting card, so our artist cut off the overlap with a sharp craft knife. Use a straight edge – such as a metal ruler – to guide you.

◀**4** Our artist decided against sizing this paper and painted straight on to it. It makes a lovely background for these autumn leaves, the dark flecks of the paper adding to the feeling of the leaves floating down from the tree.

▼ **You'll need the right equipment to transform your found materials into supports. Gather together a simple kit consisting of suitable adhesive or size, a decorator's brush, a craft knife, a pair of scissors and a ruler.**

Newspaper on cardboard

Stick it down
Stick it down

Our artist used three different adhesive solutions for mounting – PVA, Liquitex acrylic matte gel medium (both diluted with water) and wallpaper paste. All are interchangeable – you can use each of them with any of the supports shown here.

Incidentally, of all the adhesives, our artist preferred the matte gel medium – she found it made the boards and papers curl over least.

▶**1** Newsprint can be incorporated into your designs with interesting results. Newspaper is very fragile when wet, so it's important to give it the stability of a card or cardboard backing.

Wallpaper paste was the adhesive this time. Mix it up following the manufacturer's instructions, stirring it well to dissolve all the powder. The consistency should be thin enough to brush out well, yet not so thin that it drips from the brush too much.

◀**2** Apply the wallpaper paste to the back of the paper (you'll have to decide which side you want to paint on). Start from the middle, working out towards the edges, and brushing vigorously to get rid of any lumps. Once it's wet, be careful not to tear the paper.

▲**3** Position the newspaper on the card/cardboard and smooth it down from the middle outwards to dispel any air bubbles. When the surface has dried a little, put it face down on some spare paper (ensuring the surface is glue-free), and place a drawing board over it. Weight this down (with books, for example) to encourage your support to dry flat. Once it has dried completely, cut off the overlap around the edges as before.

◀**4** Although she liked the colour of the paper, our artist wanted to modify it to complement her subject. She sized this absorbent paper with dilute Liquitex matte gel medium, and mixed in some yellow acrylic paint to tone the ground.

Brown manila paper on cardboard

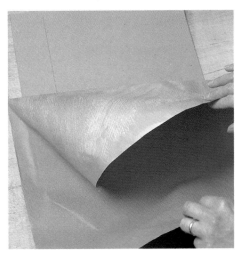

▲**1** Brown paper has a lovely colour and texture that makes a wonderful mid-toned ground for many subjects, and it's ideal for these autumn leaves. This sketchbook backing makes a sturdy support for the paper too.

▲**2** Before you get slap-happy with your brush and glue, decide which side of the paper you want to work on. Our artist chose to paint on the dull side, so she pasted the other side down on to the card/cardboard. Again, she used dilute Liquitex matte gel medium as an adhesive, brushing it out thoroughly in several different directions.

▲**3** When you stick the paper and card/cardboard together, try bending the paper in half (ensuring it doesn't crease), then place the middle of it across the middle of the card/cardboard. Roll out one side at a time smoothing out the bumps as you go. This stops air bubbles getting trapped between paper and card/cardboard.

▲**4** Once dry, turn over and cut off the overlap with a sharp craft knife. The card/cardboard was quite thick, so our artist cut the paper freehand, using the edge of the card/cardboard as a guide. If you're cutting the overlap off on the back, angle the craft knife so the tip points into the card/cardboard. This avoids an unsightly overlap on the picture side, leaving the edges clean and tidy.

▲**5** Brown paper has an organic, natural look that enhances this subject. Our artist liked it so much, she let it stand as the entire background for her picture.

Muslin on card

▶ **1** Muslin is fairly cheap and makes an excellent support. Cut a sheet of card/cardboard to size. Lay the fabric down on a flat surface and place the card/cardboard over it. Cut the muslin around the card, leaving a 1in overlap. Make sure you place the fabric so its grain runs either horizontally or vertically across the card/cardboard, rather than at an angle.

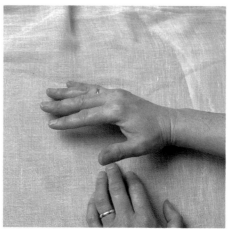

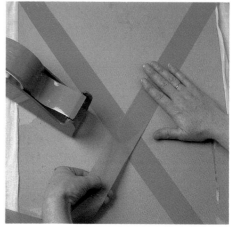

▲ **2** Our artist wanted a good strong adhesive to make sure the fabric stuck fast to the board, so she used PVA, diluting it with a little water. Apply this to the board with the decorator's brush. Brush it out well so it's even, and quite thin – if it's too thick, it will seep through the open weave of the fabric.

▲ **3** Lay the muslin on the board with the grain running horizontally or vertically across it. Smooth it from the centre outwards, working quickly to finish before the glue dries. If the fabric remains unstuck in areas, lift it up and apply more glue to the board before sticking it down again.

▲ **4** This particular card was quite thin, so our artist used brown tape to stick a cross-shape on the back to stop the edges from curling over. Stick the tape down from corner to corner and repeat on the other corners to complete the cross. Carefully cut off any overlapping tape.

◀ **5** Apply some PVA solution to the back of the card on the corners, then pull the fabric corners over the card at 45° angles and stick them down. Pull the sides over the edge of the card and stick them down in the same way (inset). Make sure you pull the fabric over tightly to leave a good, clean edge on the right side. Leave to dry.

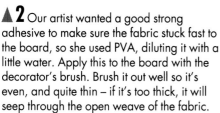

▶ **6** Painting on muslin is a little like working on a canvas, so it can be a cheap alternative. It has a lovely fabric texture so, if you're working on a large scale, you'll find it much cheaper than a huge, ready-made canvas.

Mediums for acrylic paints

Tip

There are mediums to make acrylic colours thicker or thinner, more transparent or more opaque, glossy or matt. You can even buy mediums to control the paint's drying rate.

You can greatly increase the versatility of acrylic paints by mixing them with one or more widely available acrylic mediums.

There are six main types of medium. Because acrylics are fairly new, some manufacturers may give their products different names. Read the label and ask for help in your local art shop.

Gloss medium Acrylic paints used straight from the tube dry to an eggshell finish. For a shiny finish, add gloss medium directly to the paint to thin it to a fluid consistency – but remember that mixing in water dilutes the medium, making it less glossy. If you add enough medium, the paint becomes transparent and the underlying colours shine through.

Gloss medium is ideal for applying thin layers of colour. The paint acquires depth and luminosity – qualities associated with watercolour – without loss of its adhesive properties. Gloss medium looks milky in the bottle, but dries to a transparent, shiny finish.

Experiment with different amounts of medium to find out how much to mix with the paint. Adding too much gives a more transparent layer of colour but reduces the paint's intensity.

Matt medium Like gloss, this makes the paint thinner and more fluid, but it dries to a very non-shiny finish. For a semi-gloss surface, use equal parts of matt and gloss mediums.

Because both matt and gloss mediums dry very rapidly, always keep your brushes in a jar of water when not in use. Otherwise, within a few minutes they become hard and unusable.

Flow improver Sold in bottles, this dilutes acrylic paint for maximum flow and transparency. Unlike water, it doesn't dilute the colour or reduce the paint's adhesive qualities. This makes it ideal for painting large washes of smooth

Applying mediums

Squeeze out a blob of paint on to your palette, and make a well in the middle of it. Add one or more of the mediums a little at a time, and mix thoroughly with a palette knife. If required, dilute the paint further with water, and use immediately. If you are using more than one colour plus a medium, mix the colours first, and then add the medium.

▼**Manufacturers' names for their mediums seldom leave you guessing. Be prepared, though, to do some trying and testing to achieve the effect you're after**

◀ When it's a textured finish you want for your picture, you need look no further than texture gel and modelling paste. With practice the right texture and sheen are at your fingertips.

colour. While matt and gloss mediums change the finish of the paint when dry, flow improver does not. (However, if you add too much flow improver, the paint may begin to foam, causing small bubbles to appear in the paint.)

An alternative to shop-bought flow improver is washing-up liquid/dishwasher detergent. As a general rule add one or two parts flow improver or dish washing liquid to twenty parts paint.

Retarder Acrylic paint is renowned for its incredibly fast drying rate. Retarder is a translucent gel which delays the fast-setting property of acrylic paints without most of the time affecting the consistency or colour. Depending on how much retarder you add, you can extend the paint's drying time from half an hour to as long as an entire day. Retarder is invaluable when you need to work slowly to blend colours smoothly – for example, when you want subtle gradations of skin tone in a portrait.

Experiment by adding different proportions of retarder, but don't exceed one part retarder to three parts colour because this affects the paint's consistency.

Texture gel Sometimes called gel medium, this paste-like substance thickens paint without altering its colour. It dries clear and is ideal for rich, thick brushstrokes and for impasto effects. It also increases the adhesive quality of paint, making it useful for collages.

Liquitex's acrylic texture gels offer you four formulas for easy impasto work: Ceramic Stucco, Blended Fibers, Natural Sand and Resin Sand. They have different textures and sheens. You can mix in the paint before application or paint over the dried area later.

Modelling pastes Sold in tubs and jars, modelling paste is initially thick and white. It lightens any paint it's mixed with, though, so allow for that. It has the consistency of putty and thickens the paint more than a gel medium.

Applying it to rigid surfaces such as wood or board makes a highly textured underpainting. It's best to apply a mixture of modelling paste and acrylic paint in several thinnish layers to create a thickly textured surface. Build up the surface gradually, allowing each layer to dry before adding the next. If you use only one thick layer, the paste cracks when it dries.

To make it smoother and more fluid, thin it with gloss or matt medium. Mixed 50:50 with gel medium it can be applied to flexible surfaces such as linen and cotton canvas.

YOU WILL NEED

- ☐ *20 x 16in ready primed canvas board*
- ☐ *4B graphite pencil*
- ☐ *Two flat brushes – Nos.2 and 5*
- ☐ *No.18 painting knife*
- ☐ *Cloth or paper tissue*
- ☐ *Acrylic matt medium*
- ☐ *Liquitex Natural Sand acrylic texture gel*
- ☐ *Eight colours – sap green, titanium white, yellow ochre, Payne's gray, Indo orange red, azo yellow medium, raw umber, alizarin crimson*

Autumn woodland scene

The set-up The artist used various art books and photographs for inspiration. Instead of copying one source directly, he created a work stamped and moulded with his own ideas, drawing on the sources only as reference.

▶ **1** Sketch in the tree trunks and the horizon with the 4B graphite pencil. Mix a light grey from titanium white, yellow ochre and Payne's gray, using a little acrylic matt medium and a touch of water to thin the paint to the consistency you want. Then quickly block in the tree trunks with your mix, using a No.5 brush.

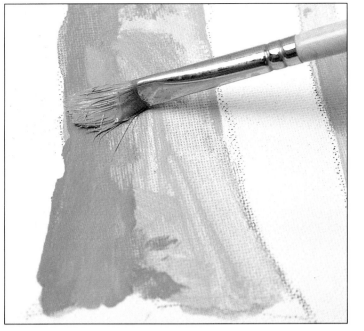

▲ **2** Darken the mix with a little more Payne's gray and paint the dark grey vertical and horizontal tones seen on some of the trunks. Add more titanium white to create light tones for the horizontal bands on a few of the trunks. Make sure the trees in the foreground are lighter than those in the background so that you gain the impression of distance.

Next, mix some raw umber, Payne's gray and yellow ochre with a tiny amount of white and matt medium and paint in the dark background. A uniform tone creates flat-looking, one-dimensional objects, so vary the degree of darkness and light to give a sense of depth. Add titanium white to the mixture to lighten it, and raw umber to darken it.

▲ **3** Mix azo yellow medium, Indo orange red and alizarin crimson with matt medium and block in the leaf-laden foreground and middleground. Scrub in this watery mixture, then leave to dry.

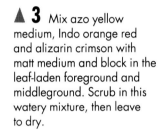

◄ **4** Then add small, thickish dabs of a mixture of azo yellow medium, Indo orange red, alizarin crimson and matt medium. This creates light and dark tones. Allow a few dabs of pure crimson to show through in some areas.
Work freely and loosely – don't worry about exact detail. Allow the whole thing to dry.

► **5** While the foreground and middleground are drying, paint in the dark tones of the background to provide greater depth. Mix some Payne's gray, sap green, yellow ochre, alizarin crimson, raw umber and titanium white (adding a touch of matt medium again), and apply with the No.2 brush. Allow the green and crimson to show through in places – you can do this by not mixing the paint too thoroughly.
Work across the horizon, adding dark and light areas to create depth.

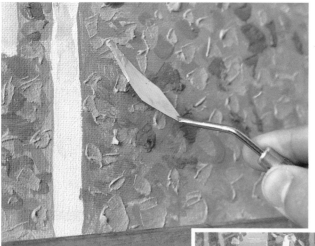

◄ **6** Mix a little Liquitex Natural Sand texture gel (or acrylic gel medium) with yellow ochre, and use the No.18 painting knife to dab on thick, generous blobs of paint in the foreground and the middleground to represent fallen leaves.

▼ **7** Add a few dabs of the same mix among the trees for the hanging and falling leaves. Allow to

▲ **8** Mix alizarin crimson, azo yellow medium and more Natural Sand texture gel. Dab on this orange mix as you did with the yellow. Don't forget to paint in the hanging leaves.

You can build up several layers of texture in this way until you're satisfied with the result.

▼ **9** The final painting glows with autumnal colour and there are plenty of interesting textures and tones to provide a three-dimensional woodland landscape. Notice the vertical brushstrokes in the middle, leading the eye up from the foreground into the distance.

Matt medium gives a soft look to the surface – it goes well with the autumn theme.

PART 2

Creative Techniques

The versatility of acrylics

With fast-drying acrylic paints, you have the opportunity to work loosely and expressively as well as going for pin-point details – all in one sitting.

Because acrylic paints dry so fast, they are one of the most versatile media to work with, allowing you to block in large areas and make fine details easily at the same time. (With oils you have to work in stages, allowing time for the paint surface to dry slightly, otherwise you will find that you are simply moving the paint around.)

Even thick acrylic impasto forms a skin quickly, allowing you to overpaint in minutes. Adding one or more of the mediums available – gloss and matt mediums, texture gels and pastes, and flow improvers – increases the paint's versatility even further.

Creating the right combination of detail and loose, gestural brushwork is important – you don't want the foreground and background competing for attention with the main subject. In our artist's demonstration painting of two Spitfires, for example, he applied the paint loosely and expressively for the sky and the foliage, scumbling and blending colours with his fingers, then used a fine brush to paint the details of the planes with precision. Even the insignia have been carefully rendered.

The set-up Our artist based his painting on photos which he took at an air show. Use our finished painting to help you, or find suitable pictures in books or magazines to use as references. Better still, try to visit an air show for yourself!

▲**1** Draw the composition on the canvas with your 2B pencil. Then mix a large quantity of gloss medium and water (roughly half and half). Mix this with your paints to intensify the colours and give the finished painting a slight shine.

Block in the planes with a mix of dilute gloss medium, Mars black and light violet. Combine the dilute gloss medium with Mars black and varying amounts of Hooker's green to block in the land. Allow to dry.

◄**2** Paint in the sky with a dilute mix of cobalt blue and titanium white, using your 1 in flat brush. Blot occasionally with a cotton rag to create texture in the sky.

▲**3** Add white and light violet to vary the tones across the sky. Make broad, free strokes, and use your fingers to blend the paint, adding a touch of Mars black to create rain clouds. Don't worry at this point if you lose the edges of the plane – you can redefine them later on.

▶**4** Fill in the dark areas on the upper plane with a mix of Mars black and cobalt blue. The point of your No.3 round brush is perfect for capturing fine details, such as the cockpit and the tail. Mix titanium white with just a touch of Mars black to create a light grey for the blur of the moving propeller.

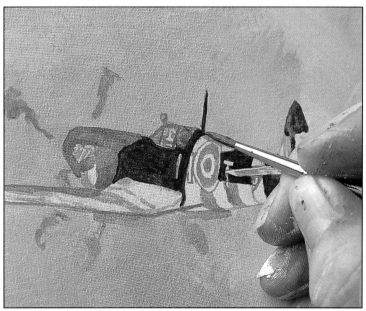

◀**5** Add a little Mars black and cobalt blue to the top plane's propeller and blend it with your finger to suggest movement. Paint the edge of the wings and the undercarriage with Mars black mixed with dilute gloss medium, and fill in the lighter tones of the plane with light violet and the grey you mixed in step 1. Notice how the plane takes on a metallic look. Allow to dry.

Continue to add details to the top plane. Use your No.3 brush loaded with alizarin crimson toned down with a tiny amount of Mars black to fill in the reddish target insignia on the fuselage and fin. Paint the yellow circle around the insignia with cadmium yellow, and use titanium white for the lettering.

Mix dioxazine purple, Mars black and a little dilute gloss medium to rework all the darkest areas, such as the wheels and undercarriage.

◀ **6** Apply more white and cobalt blue to the sky with the 1in flat brush, and use the cotton rag to work into the paint, moving it about and blotting some areas. Add a little violet, and blend the paint with your fingers. Use a more dilute paint solution around the lower plane, again blotting with the rag where necessary.

Let yourself go to create a loose, expressive sky with lots of character.

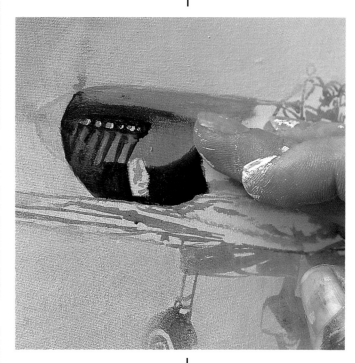

▲ **7** Mix cobalt blue and white for the top of the lower plane. Use the No.3 brush. Add the exhausts with black, and blend the two colours slightly. Add some dilute gloss medium, cobalt blue and black, and work back across the body and side panels.

▲ **8** Apply blackish grey details to the lower plane's nose cone. Add some dioxazine purple and a little Hooker's green to enrich the black areas. Paint the red insignia with alizarin crimson toned down with Mars black, then use titanium white for the number and letter on the fuselage.

▶ **9** Fill in the wing with light blue (cobalt blue and white). Add black to this mix to make a dark grey, and work over the darkest areas of the wing.

Continue working on the sky with blues and whites made from cobalt blue and white.

◄ 10 Work on the cockpit and pilot. Use cadmium yellow and white for details and Mars black for the undercarriage and wheels. Lighten the wheel centres with a grey mix. Detail the stripes under the plane's tail, darkening the black with purple as they curve under. Follow the form of the plane with your brushstrokes. Shade the white stripes too, as they turn under the plane.

Tip

Means to an end
Remember, brushes are simply tools – a means to an end. If you can achieve the results you want more effectively without them, don't use them! Our artist favoured rags and fingers in this painting for subtle blending effects.

► 11 Mix Mars black with dioxazine purple, and paint in the dark areas of the tail. Add the fin with a mid-tone grey (mixed from Mars black and titanium white with a little cobalt blue). Put in black stripes over the fin, and blend the colours with your finger. Use a lighter grey on the tailplane.

► 12 Add the colour details on the tail's insignia with the same colours you used on the fuselage. The Spitfires are now starting to look extremely realistic – notice how three-dimensional they appear.

13 Now begin work on the trees and land with Hooker's green darkened slightly with a touch of dioxazine purple. Scrub on the colour loosely, twisting and turning your 1in brush; then blot areas with the rag. Scratch into the foliage with your brush handle for texture if you wish.

14 Mix a dark green with Hooker's green and burnt sienna and use it to darken some areas of the bushes to provide tonal contrasts. Block in the grassy area along the runway with yellow oxide, titanium white and Hooker's green. Again, vary your mixes (some light, others dark) to provide depth. Also vary your brushstrokes to add interest and a fresh look. Don't try to render details but aim to make the foliage loose and expressive.

15 For the runway's dark greys, mix cobalt blue, titanium white, Mars black, dioxazine purple and dilute gloss medium in various proportions and make long, smooth horizontal strokes with your 1in flat brush.

With the same brush, apply Hooker's green randomly in front of the bushes to suggest growth. Touch in a little grey and yellow ochre under the bushes, blotting areas with a damp rag. Mix some Acra gold and yellow ochre, and flick it in sharp strokes to add more colour to this area.

16 Make a yellow-green with Hooker's green, yellow ochre and white, and use flicking strokes with your No.5 brush in many directions to suggest grass in front of the runway. Again, alter the proportions of the colours to vary the tones.

◀ **17** Paint the lower plane's indistinct shadow on the runway with a mix of cobalt blue and Mars black. Blend this smoothly with your 1in flat brush.

▼ **18** Add any last-minute details, such as the lower plane's aerial, with Mars black. Tone down the blur of the upper plane's propeller with a little titanium white, applied with your finger, and add the propeller blur on the lower plane in the same way you did for the upper plane.

Sky, land and runway have been painted loosely and expressively to give the impression of a bright, breezy day. Yet the details on the planes – veterans of World War II – are spot-on. The artist captured the scene in one sitting with great energy and spirit.

Washes, spatters & puddles

Traditional watercolour techniques can add a new dimension to acrylic painting. The medium's ability to dry fast means that subsequent layers will not muddy its colours or disturb its lines.

Acrylics can be used in much the same way as traditional watercolours. However, unlike watercolours, which remain soluble and tend to mix with subsequent layers, acrylics dry permanently – they are not re-soluble in water. This allows the artist to build up layers of transparent colour to achieve extremely subtle effects. The transparent quality of acrylic (when used as watercolour), means that it's advisable for beginners to stick to the tried and tested watercolour maxim of working light to dark.

Acrylics tend to be brighter than their watercolour equivalents, so you may find it helps to test your washes on a piece of paper first. Most watercolour techniques are possible with acrylics.

In the painting demonstrated here, the most important of these was to allow paint to puddle in some areas to suggest the contours of the car. Remember to allow each layer to dry before applying the next. Gently playing a hair dryer over the surface is a useful way of speeding up this process. But be careful not to blow wet paint into places you don't want it to go.

◀ **The set-up** Our artist decided that acrylics were the ideal medium to depict a classic car in a desert setting.

He decided to use the paint thin, and, as with watercolour, to leave the white of the paper support to describe the highlights on the bumpers and headlamps. Other watercolour techniques he called into play include wet-on-dry washes, puddling and spattering.

◀**1** Lightly sketch all the main elements of the subject with the HB pencil. Use the No.10 round brush to paint the sky with a wash of cobalt blue and a touch of ultramarine. Turn the board upside down so that the washes travel in the right direction. Roll the brush around the white clouds to break up the clean edges of the wash.

Use this blue mix with the No.6 brush to work in all the areas of blue which are reflected in the car window and the chrome. Tilt the board so the paint puddles at the bottom of the washes, suggesting darker reflections. Add a little alizarin crimson to your mix. Use this around the bumper and blend it in to the wet area.

YOU WILL NEED

- [ ] A 15 X 22in sheet of 200lb NOT Bockingford/cold pressed watercolour paper, stretched and taped to a board
- [ ] A table easel
- [ ] HB pencil
- [ ] A palette for acrylics
- [ ] Two jars of water
- [ ] Kitchen roll
- [ ] A hair dryer
- [ ] Two round brushes: a No.10 and a No.6
- [ ] Nine Liquitex acrylics: yellow oxide, alizarin crimson hue, cadmium red light, naphthol crimson, cobalt blue, ultramarine blue, sap green, burnt sienna and Payne's gray

◀ **2** Use a very watery mix of yellow oxide and the No.10 brush to wash over the rocks and car. After the last wash has dried, add a little cadmium red light to the mix. Use this to paint over the car to give it a slight pinkness. Add a little more cadmium red light to the wash to redden the foreground and also to paint in the darker area of the far headlamp (see step 4).

Add more yellow oxide and cadmium red light to your mix to create an orange. Use this to paint over the rocks, leaving out the lighter areas.

▶ **3** Add a little more cadmium red light to the mix and work over the roof of the car. Wet the car's rusty areas with clean water and add a little burnt sienna to the red-orange mix. Flood this into the wet areas. When dry, the resulting watermarks describe perfectly the worn paintwork on the car.

▼ **4** By varying the ratio of paint to water, you can mix different tones of orange. Work across the rocks, alternating lighter and darker colours to suggest contours. Add the car's red badge, the shadows between the radiator bars and the shadows and writing on the number plate. Take the No.6 brush and spatter a little of this mix over the left of the car's bodywork and over the bonnet/hood to suggest rust.

▶ **5** Using the same varied orange mixes as before, work over the rocks once more, building up form as you overlay washes. Allow the rocks to dry, and darken the intensity of one of the orange mixes with cadmium red light. Use the No.6 brush once more to spatter over the rocks. Protect the sky with your free hand or a torn piece of paper.

◀ **6** See how the spattering adds interest and texture to the rocks. Continue to spatter over the lower foreground – this helps to liven up the picture. Don't worry if some spatters bleed into the wet paper. They may look obvious at this stage, but as these areas are developed they become much less noticeable.

▶ **7** Make a mix using sap green, ultramarine and Payne's gray. Use this to work over the bonnet/hood, wetting areas with clean water and dropping in colour. The colour bleeds through and gives the appearance of peeling and distressed paintwork. Use the mix to work around the headlights and 'draw' in the contours of the bonnet/hood.

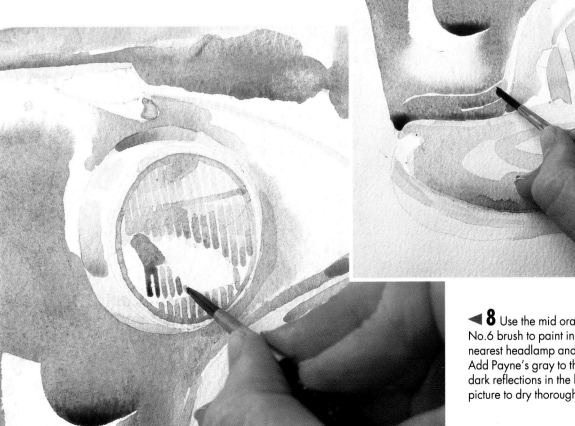

◀ **8** Use the mid orange mix and the No.6 brush to paint in the lines on the nearest headlamp and fill in the hub cap. Add Payne's gray to the mix and detail the dark reflections in the lamp. Leave the picture to dry thoroughly.

▲9 Add some naphthol crimson and a little ultramarine to the darker orange mix. Work over the rocks, really pulling out their shadowed, craggy areas. Do a little more spattering with this dark colour to suggest a pock-marked surface.

Mix some Payne's gray and ultramarine and carefully outline the windscreen and headlamps. Work over the chrome, stroking in the dark reflections with this deep colour. Also use some for the shadow of the number plate.

▲10 All the light and mid tones are now in place so you can begin working on the darkest colours and tones. The picture now begins to develop depth and sparkle as these darker areas are painted in.

Use a dark mixture of Payne's gray and a little naphthol crimson to paint the dark areas inside the car (see step 12), and paint the shadows under the car, not forgetting the ones around the wheels.

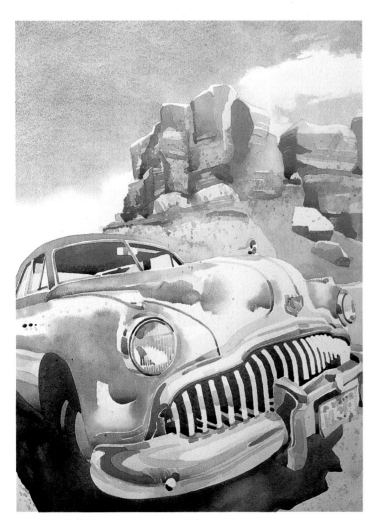

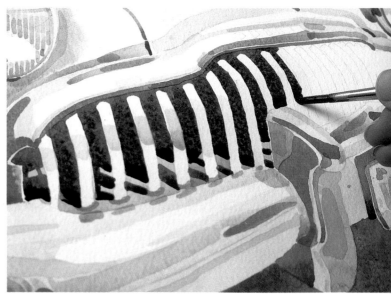

▲11 Carefully paint through the radiator grille with the same mix, leaving slanting orange highlights inside. These help suggest the light passing through the grille and create an excellent three-dimensional effect.

◄12 Allow the painting to dry. Then stand back to assess the work so far. Mix some Payne's gray and a little naphthol crimson to darken some tones on the chrome.

◀ **13** Mix some sap green, a little ultramarine and some Payne's gray. Use this to intensify the colour on the bonnet. While the area is still wet, mix some naphthol crimson and Payne's gray and paint in the shadow under the headlamp. See how our artist let the colour pool here to create a really deep tone which conveys the shape of the car. Try placing the board at a slight angle, so the wet paint settles at the bottom of the shadow's curve where the colour is deepest.

Using the No.6 brush, carefully run a dark line over the top of the radiator.

◀ **14** Use cobalt blue and a touch of ultramarine to intensify the blue reflections in the bumper and across the radiator grille. Vary the tone of this blue by strengthening the mix.

Develop the radiator further and detail the reflections in the chrome. Darken the inside of the window with Payne's gray and a little naphthol crimson. Then use the same mix to work around the edges of the bonnet and on the headlamp. Also work on the tyre, and darken the shadow under the front bumper.

Tip

Quick fix
Remember that acrylics are not water-soluble when dry, so if you make a mistake it must be corrected while the paint is still wet. Don't panic! Carefully blot off the paint with plenty of clean kitchen roll, then continue painting.

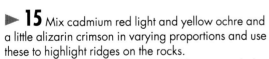

▶ **15** Mix cadmium red light and yellow ochre and a little alizarin crimson in varying proportions and use these to highlight ridges on the rocks.

To lift the painting, some more colour is needed in the sky. Use an intense mix of cobalt blue and ultramarine to work across this area. Turn your board upside down if it makes it easier to paint.

Tip

White out
Our artist didn't include any white on his palette because it's a very opaque paint and would make his mixes opaque — he wanted his washes to be transparent, like watercolour. However, if you want to lighten a tone which is too dark or to cover a mistake, you can take advantage of white's opacity by adding it to a mix to cover the paint layer underneath.

► **16** As a final touch, use a deep orange mix to paint a line across the bumper to warm the colour there. Make any other adjustments you think necessary. Our artist put a little more orange 'rust' on top of the bonnet/hood, for example.

The finished painting demonstrates the colourful and bold effect that acrylic paints can have when used like watercolours. The composition is further enlivened by the drastically foreshortened perspective of the car. The artist's use of spattering and watermarks has also added texture to the picture.

Using a limited palette

You don't need many acrylic colours to begin painting. Using a limited palette helps you become familiar with your colours and their mixes, and it also holds the composition together.

There are dozens of acrylic colours on the market today – not just the more traditional ones like Payne's gray and ultramarine, but also wild pearlescent and metallic silvers, burning-bright yellows and oranges and many others. Even the spectrum of landscape colours is vast.

Most beginners make the mistake of buying far too many acrylic colours. You simply don't need them. In fact, if you have a wide range of colours at your disposal, you'll probably spend a lot of time deliberating about colour selection instead of dealing with their application or improving your compositional skills. The colours you choose for your limited palette depend on your subject – for example, a palette for landscapes is likely to be completely different from one for portraits, and even for portraits it depends on the sitter's skin colour.

Restricting your palette to four or five colours helps to unify the whole composition. You can find hints of the five colours our artist used in his demonstration all over the painting – and they contribute an important sense of harmony to the whole picture. You can also mix a number of other colours from the basic palette to create different tones, helping you to become familiar with your colours and their mixes.

In our artist's painting, the medium density fibreboard (MDF) is left unpainted in places, where it provides an excellent mid-tone for the dried leaves of the reedmace. And the colour and texture of the board shine through the thin wash of colour laid down for the still water in the middleground, creating the effect of a shimmering, reflective surface.

► Using only a limited palette of six colours – yellow ochre, French ultramarine, burnt umber, burnt sienna, titanium white and philo green – the artist has achieved great depth and variety.
'Trafalgar Square' by Richard Smith, 1988, acrylic on hardboard, 30½ x 20½in

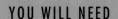

Reedmace in the lake margins

The set-up Our artist combined elements from two photographs of reedmace in a lake in Bedfordshire. A close-up of some reedmace served as the main reference, but he introduced the simple background from his second photo to balance his composition and reflect foreground colour.

YOU WILL NEED

- One sheet of 30 x 20in (6mm thick) medium density fibreboard (MDF)
- Four brushes – a No.9 long flat, a No. 9 short flat, a No.6 round and a 2in decorators' brush
- One 50mm (2in) long painting knife
- Palette knife
- Two jars of water
- Disposable palette
- Sponge
- Water sprayer
- Acrylic matt medium
- Five acrylic colours – burnt umber, yellow ochre, ultramarine, titanium white and burnt sienna

1 Mix ultramarine and white on your palette with the painting knife, and spread a narrow band of colour along the top edge of the board for the sky. Then paint the distant bank of the lake with a rough mix of yellow ochre, white and slight touches of burnt umber; suggest the outline of trees and bushes with the tip of the knife.

Now paint the lake using loose mixes of ultramarine, white and touches of burnt umber, leaving the pigment virtually pure in places and letting the board show through in others. Make sweeping horizontal strokes. The edge of the knife is useful for suggesting different wave patterns (inset).

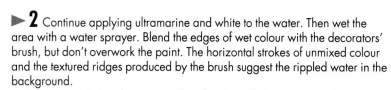

2 Continue applying ultramarine and white to the water. Then wet the area with a water sprayer. Blend the edges of wet colour with the decorators' brush, but don't overwork the paint. The horizontal strokes of unmixed colour and the textured ridges produced by the brush suggest the rippled water in the background.

Continue painting the water with pale mixes of ultramarine and white. Make horizontal strokes back and forth across the board with the same brush, spraying on a little more water if needed. Apply the paint thinly like a glaze, letting the warm tone of the board show here and there. Add more blue, then burnt umber as you move down to the foreground. Leave it to dry.

◄ 3 Here our artist turned both painting and photo upside down to help him paint what his eye was really seeing, rather than what he expected to see. It also forced him to concentrate on a detail, without distraction from the overall composition.

Use loose mixes of yellow ochre, white and touches of burnt umber to establish the lighter tones of the reedmace. Make long, vertical strokes with the painting knife in some areas, short dabs in others.

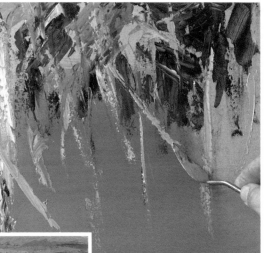

Tip

Spreading paint

Adjust the nozzle on the water atomizer to spray a fine mist (test it out a few times, pointing somewhere other than your painting!). Then pull the trigger two or three times over the lake area (top).

This makes colour blending quick and easy (above). It also thins the paint, allowing you to see parts of the board in places.

▲ 4 Here you can see the subtle yet realistic colour mixes the artist used to suggest the dense clumps of reeds. Still working with the painting upside down, take up small, individual dollops of yellow ochre, white, burnt umber and ultramarine and apply them to the board. Allow them to blend as you work loosely and freely with the knife, creating smooth areas as well as ridges – these help to suggest individual stems and leaves.

Load the edge of the painting knife with a loose mix of yellow ochre, white and touches of burnt umber, and form the long stems. Allow the painting to dry thoroughly.

◄ 5 Notice how our artist has built up texture and tone by placing some angled slabs of colour next to others and some over each other. There are light areas over dark ones, and vice versa. A few diagonal stems complement and add interest to the composition, and they break the uniformity of the vertical stems, providing a sense of balance.

60

6 Mix yellow ochre and white, and paint the reedmace heads with your No.9 long flat brush. Firmly push the brush on to the board as you drag the paint down. This creates soft, feathery effects. Add burnt umber to your mix and use it to darken some of the heads.

Load the No.9 short flat with plenty of titanium white, and make a few dabs and brushstrokes on the palette to compress the brush bristles into a neat, compact head. Now paint the spikes on the male heads by carefully touching the brush to the board (inset). Re-form the brush shape after each mark.

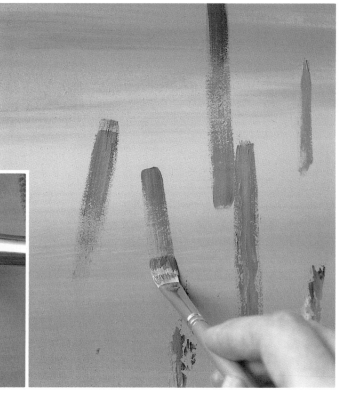

7 Using the No.9 short flat, paint the darkest foreground tones with mixes of burnt umber and ultramarine. Allow the brown to dominate the mix in some areas, and the ultramarine to dominate in others, to provide a sense of depth.

Paint quickly, with short, vertical strokes of colour, pushing the brush bristles hard against the board. As you move back into the reeds, drag a dryish brush over the ground to give a misty effect, creating a sense of perspective.

8 Now add pale impasto paint to the flowerheads. This will bring these areas forward. For the distant reedmace on the right, dab on small marks in a pale, thick mix of white and yellow ochre. Let yourself go – twist and flick the brush on the board to produce interesting textures.

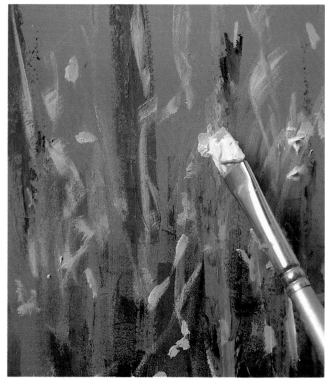

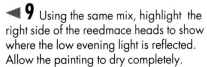 **9** Using the same mix, highlight the right side of the reedmace heads to show where the low evening light is reflected. Allow the painting to dry completely.

▼ **10** Pour a few teaspoons of acrylic matt medium into a jar and mix it well with the same amount of water. On your palette, mix burnt sienna with this glazing medium in equal proportions, and then loosely glaze over the reedmace with the No.9 long flat. Scrub on the translucent colour with rough strokes in several different directions.

This glaze warms up the reedmace and creates the effect of rich evening light. The uneven application makes for different intensities of warmth, giving the impression of shimmering light.

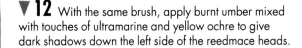 **11** To build up the pale tones of the stems and to define their form further, add small strokes and dots of white (mixed with a little yellow ochre) with the No.6 round brush. Use the tip of the brush for fine detail and the whole brush for some bolder lines. Don't be afraid to apply the paint quite thickly in places.

▼ **12** With the same brush, apply burnt umber mixed with touches of ultramarine and yellow ochre to give dark shadows down the left side of the reedmace heads.

◀ **13** Our artist strengthened the distance between the reeds and the water by darkening the area where the two merge with a mix of ultramarine and burnt umber. Then, using grey-brown mixes of ultramarine, yellow ochre and titanium white, he added small dots of colour over the dark tone. Allow this to dry thoroughly.

With the same glazing mix you used in step 10, glaze the lower half of the painting. Use a large sponge to apply the colour fairly evenly to the reedmace and immediate vicinity of the lake. Leave the paint to dry.

▲ **14** Re-establish the light tones over the glaze with the No.6 brush. Use dry mixes of white with a little yellow ochre added, applying the paint boldly and thickly in dots, dabs and some longer strokes.

◀ **15** Stand back from your painting to assess it. You may want to emphasize the dark tone between the reeds and the water with a wet mix of ultramarine, white and a touch of burnt umber, painting small dots of colour among the stems.

Because the glazes have the effect of warming and muting the colours, you may find you need to lighten the foreground further. Don't be nervous when applying the paint quite thickly in this area. Virtually pure white pigment with just a touch of yellow ochre achieves a dramatic effect.

Monochrome underpainting

A monochrome underpainting allows you to organize your picture from the word go, so you can respond freely to your subject when it comes to applying colour.

If you want to give your painting a really good start, especially if you're a beginner, then make a monochrome underpainting (known technically as *grisaille*). It's very similar to making tonal studies. You use one colour to organize the tones in your subject before you start to think about local colours. This avoids the confusion that can easily arise when you try to depict the colours and tones of an object in one go (an area in which many beginners fall down). Sorting out the underlying tonal structure of your subject early on – the positions of those vital lights and darks – can lead to a much more successful final result.

And once you've done the underpainting, you get a monochrome preview of your painting. This allows you the chance to look at how the composition works, and see if it's balanced correctly. At this stage you have the freedom to redraw until it's accurate. Later on, you obliterate the underpainting anyway. The monochrome underpainting means you can respond freely to what you see without worrying about the vital aspects you've already dealt with. For some artists, it's a good way of systematically organizing a painting from the start. Others would say it's saving the best until last!

▼ The monochrome underpainting (left) looks very different from the finished picture (right). But if you squint at them you'll see the similarities – tonally they are almost identical. Once our artist had established the tones with Payne's gray, she was free to enjoy the rich application of colour.

YOU WILL NEED

- One 23 x 20in canvas board
- Easel
- Thin stick of charcoal
- Two bristle brushes: No.12 long flat and No.6 round; two synthetic acrylic brushes: No.3 round and No.6 long flat
- Two jars of water
- Tear away paper palette; ruler
- Nine acrylic colours; Payne's gray, burnt umber, cadmium yellow, alizarin crimson, cadmium red, permanent green, phthalo green, cerulean blue, titanium white

Keep responding

This demonstration shows how much a painting can change in appearance as it progresses. This isn't because the artist corrected mistakes, but because she responded directly to what she saw, making adjustments as she noticed new things.

When your painting begins to take shape, let it 'talk back to you' by taking ideas from the painting itself, as well as your subject. This enjoyable experience is often spoiled for the novice whose concern all along is how the final painting will look. Put aside preconceptions and simply look – you may surprise yourself with your finished work.

Establishing the structure in a monochrome underpainting gives you freedom for spontaneity with your brushwork, colours and ideas, and allows you to concentrate on adding that magical personal touch.

▲**1** Sketch the composition with your stick of charcoal. Make the proportions as accurate as you can, especially the ellipses of the lamp – they get deeper and more pronounced as they move farther down from the eye level. Draw a vertical line running down through the middle of the lamp to help you make it symmetrical. Indicate the cupboard and the books on the shelf in simple blocks.

▶**2** Start by assessing all the tones. Hood your eyes and look for lights and darks. Put these in with your No.12 long flat brush, using dilute Payne's gray with more or less water for the various tones. Start with the table. Its dark surface is lighter where the lamp reflects on it, so leave this area blank.

In the study

The set-up The focal point – the paraffin lamp – was the main light source in this still life. To suggest moving light, the artist worked in the classical system of 'lost and found edges'. Instead of making hard edges, you avoid working precisely around edges, letting them 'find themselves' as the painting develops.

◀**3** Continue working in this way, depicting all the tones you see. Think about the shapes of the shadows too – they help to make the painting more interesting. The angular shadow under the cupboard contrasts well with the rounded lamp.

▼**4** Compare one tone with another and build them up slowly and thoughtfully. For example, use the darkness of the table to show you how light the book should be.

◀ **5** Keep building up the underpainting, assessing tones and deepening them where necessary. Continue until you're completely happy with your work. Allow the underpainting to dry.

▶ **6** Now begin to paint the local colours. Start with dilute washes that stain the support. You can slowly build up the painting on these.

Apply dilute alizarin crimson to the background area around the lamp, using your No.6 round brush. Notice how, although the same wash is used above and below the bookshelf, it looks much darker below because of the tonal underpainting. Paint the edge of the cupboard door with a wash of burnt umber. Use very dilute phthalo green for the lampshade.

▼ **7** Using the same brush, paint the table top with burnt umber, enriching it with alizarin crimson. Use dilute cadmium yellow for the lamp stand. The underpainting turns this into quite a cool, greenish yellow which suggests the reflection of the light. Add the dark reflections of the table top to the lamp stand with the colour you just used on the table.

Paint the book with dilute alizarin crimson, adding white and cadmium yellow for the highlight (see inset). For this, use your No.6 long flat.

▲ **8** Now start to use your paint thicker, diluting it with less water. Put in the background area around the lamp with a mixture of alizarin crimson, cadmium yellow and titanium white, using loose, general strokes. Add warmer reflections to the lamp stand with cadmium red and cadmium yellow.

Tip

Use your ruler
Hold a ruler firmly in your free hand and rest your brush against it, sliding it up

or down the edge to paint a straight line. This steadying guide is useful for those lines that need to be as straight as you can make them.

10 Use cadmium yellow for the bold areas of colour on the lamp stand. Put a dab of yellow on the table to suggest the lamp reflecting on the table top. Fill the blank area on the table – which you left for the lamp's reflection – with dilute cadmium yellow.

Add cerulean blue to the background mix for the area around the lamp, using smoother strokes for a more even coverage.

9 Paint more warm reflections on the lamp stand with burnt umber. Use the table mixture plus alizarin crimson to deepen the colour of the table top. Notice how the lamp stand edges are left vague so you can't see where the table ends and the lamp stand begins.

Mix phthalo green and white for the greenish tinge on the lampshade. Apply this loosely with your No.6 round brush, covering the outside edge.

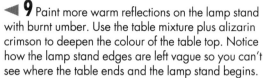

11 Using the same brush, paint the curtain on the right with permanent green. Our artist used her different mixes to put dabs of colour on the books and cupboard. All objects pick up colours from their surroundings, so train your eye to look for these. The left side of the cupboard takes direct light from the lampshade, so use the lampshade colour to paint it.

12 Using your finger, apply titanium white to the lampshade to tone down the green a little. Load the paint on thickly to make rich, fresh marks. Our artist also decided to tone down the yellow on the lamp stand with a little burnt umber.

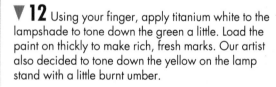

◄ 13 Mix cerulean blue and titanium white, warmed with a little alizarin crimson. Scrub this on to the background area to the right of the lamp with your No.12 flat brush. This murky mix helps to lead the eye away from the brightness of the lamp, into the background. And by painting up to the edge of the lamp, you give its shape more definition. Apply brilliant strips of alizarin crimson and cadmium yellow to the books on the shelf.

The overall mood of the painting emerges now – warm and energetic, with a shimmering surface.

Tip

Thumbs up

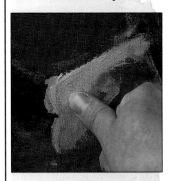

Fingers and thumbs make excellent painting tools. The book and its reflection on the table (see step 16) are right next to each other, giving you the opportunity to use closely related colours. To make an impression of the two merged forms, blend their shapes with your thumb. It's the perfect shape for painting the rounded spine too.

► 14 Mix phthalo green, white and a touch of cadmium yellow for a brisk attack with your No.12 flat brush to suggest the rounded shape of the lampshade. Again, don't worry about the edge – you'll deal with that later. Build up a little more detail on the lamp stand using a mix of cadmium yellow, burnt umber and alizarin crimson.

▼ 15 Study the lamp stand to pick out the subtleties of colour. The green reflections become bluish towards the base; the yellow gets very warm in the middle; the sides reflect the warm red table top. Add the yellow highlights with hard edges to echo the texture of the brass. Use the colours you've already put on the lamp stand, darkening them with burnt umber.

Create a variety of colours mixed from titanium white, alizarin crimson, cerulean blue, burnt umber, and Payne's gray to build up the books on the shelf.

◄ 16 Paint the book's reflection on the table using a mix of titanium white with alizarin crimson and Payne's gray. (See Tip above.)

Paint a crisp red line for the edge of the shelf – mix alizarin crimson with enough water to make it flow easily and use a ruler to keep your hand steady (See Tip on the opposite page.)

Bring on the lamp stand with the colours you've already used to add more details. Add lively brushwork to the table top using cerulean blue with a little phthalo green and white. Use cerulean blue along the bottom of the shelf, adding white for the energetic shadow to the left of the books.

Mix a pale yellow to give the lampshade an edge. Make sure you don't obliterate the greenish tint.

▶ **17** With your No.3 brush, give the books more definition by painting straight lines, using Payne's gray to suggest their edges. Rest your brush on a ruler to help you get the lines straight.

▼ **18** When the paint has dried, put in the glass chimney on the lamp. Use varying mixtures of titanium white, alizarin crimson, cerulean blue, burnt umber and Payne's gray to suggest the distorted shapes of the books seen through the glass.

Once this has dried, put a little titanium white on the edge of your ruler with a brush and press it on to the surface of your painting, making crisp lines that suggest the edge of the chimney and the highlight. Use more titanium white to tidy up the lampshade and give the top more shape and detail. Put a little dot of red from your palette on the lampshade to suggest a reflected highlight from the table.

▶ **19** The finished painting has a cosy warmth with a variety of rich pinks and reds. The feeling of moving, shimmering light is captured through all the sparkling reflections and fleeting dabs of colour. The many changes in the course of the painting, as the artist responded to the new things she saw, create a successful painting without ever altering the underlying tonal structure provided by the monochrome underpainting.

Glazing with acrylic

The technique of glazing helps you achieve a wide range of subtle – and beautiful – effects with acrylic paints.

Glazing with oil paints to build up layers of colour – some opaque, some transparent – is a technique developed by the Old Masters. They produced paintings with a depth and subtlety impossible to achieve by any other means. And that is very much what you can do today when glazing with modern acrylic paint.

Acrylic is wonderful for glazing simply because it dries so quickly. You have all the advantages of the technique with only a fraction of the waiting time necessary with oil paints.

What is a glaze?

A glaze is a thin film of transparent colour laid over a dried underpainting. You can put a single glaze on top of a finished painting to give an overall unifying effect, or you can build up colour

and tone with film after film of transparent paint, allowing each layer to dry thoroughly before applying the next.

Building up paint like this creates a final surface colour that is a complex combination of all the layers and gives your finished painting great depth and luminosity.

Using glazes

Glazing is suitable for almost any subject, but it is particularly good for portraits and figure painting. Here successive glazes help you to achieve delicate modulations of tone and colour that result in lively, fresh skin hues.

Shadows, too, are excellent subjects for glazing. Many people start by painting shadows as black or dark patches of colour, but if you look

▲ **Glazing is a marvellous technique for describing the translucency of water. You can use many thin glazes, one over another, to build up a feeling of depth and catch the reflection of light on the surface.**

The sequence of glazes perfectly captures the shifting, elusive qualities that make water such a challenge for artists.

'Dipper by the stream' by Richard Smith , acrylic on board, 17 x 27in

Trying out colours

Different colours act differently. Chromium oxide is opaque...

... while phthalo green is much more transparent.

Chromium oxide mixed with water is a little transparent.

Phthalo green mixed with water is highly transparent.

This is chromium oxide laid over cadmium yellow.

This is phthalo green laid over cadmium yellow.

carefully you can see they have many colours – and great depth as well. If you block in opaque colour and then overlay it with several layers of glaze your shadow areas become much more realistic and interesting.

Of course, there are many other applications for glazes, especially if you want to create a certain mood or if your painting needs some help to 'hang' together.

For example, you may decide that the sky in a landscape is too cool, but adding another layer of paint would be too drastic. If you mix a glaze of ochre and apply it thinly over the area near the horizon you can give the sky a delicate blush of warmer colour.

Again, if you start by blocking in the main features of your painting as patches of colour and then work them up, the colours in the final image may not 'sit comfortably' with each other. Applying a glaze of a suitable tint over the whole painting helps pull the picture together so all the different elements harmonize pleasantly.

Another use for glazing is to define space in a painting. If the background of a landscape is 'coming forward' too much, lay a pale blue or blue-grey glaze over it to unite all the background elements and 'knock' them back into the distance where they belong.

Glazing with acrylics

The simplest way to make an acrylic glaze is to thin the paint with water. Another way is to add some matt or gloss medium. These extend the paint and make it flow more easily, so it covers the surface but doesn't retain the mark of the brush.

A glaze made with water, or with a matt medium, dries to a matt finish. A glaze made with water can be used for washes that resemble watercolour, or for laying in an underpainting. A gloss medium creates a glaze which is more translucent than those made with water or matt medium, and it dries to an attractive sheen.

Working with glazes

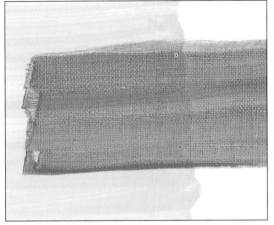

▲ With acrylic glazes you usually work from light to dark for subtle colour effects and a sense of depth. Cadmium red over cadmium yellow makes a good orange.

▲ Glazes need to be thin so the colour beneath shows through – you can use water for your initial glazes, then move on to a matt or gloss medium for the final layers.

Mixing and using different glazes require some practice. Only then can you see how all the various colours affect each other. You usually work from light to dark – laying glazes of transparent colour in increasingly darker tints over a dry underpainting of a paler colour. In this way you gradually build up tone and colour (much as you do in watercolour). It's a good idea to test your glaze mixtures on a sheet of paper – useful if you need to recreate mixtures later on.

But you can also use a pale glaze to modify a darker colour (although you can't obliterate underlying colour with transparent paint). For example, you could give an area of Payne's gray a bluer tinge with a glaze of cerulean blue, or warm it up a little with raw sienna.

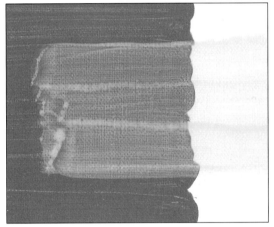

▲ A pale glaze painted over a darker colour can modify it to some extent. Here a glaze of cadmium yellow over cadmium red gives a subtle orange tinge.

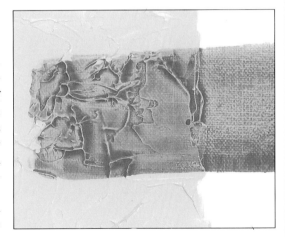

▲ You can also apply a glaze over a textured underpainting to bring out the irregularities of the surface and modify the colour as well.

◄ **2** With the tip of the knife apply more cadmium red and crimson to paint the back and shoulders of the bird, allowing the black of the board to show through in places. Mix ultramarine and burnt umber to make a black for the lower head area.

Mix cerulean blue with a little white and yellow ochre, and paint the main back area. Create the long tail feathers with a mix of naphthol crimson and a touch of yellow ochre and cerulean blue. Make long, sweeping knife marks, adding more blue towards the tip of the tail.

► **3** Use a mixture of ultramarine and burnt umber (which makes a rich black) to tidy up and redefine the edges of the tail feathers.

▲ **4** Mix cerulean blue and azo yellow medium with a palette knife (but not too thoroughly) for the green back – apply the paint with the tip of the large knife, making short angular jabs.

To cover the large area of the wing (and also the back) as quickly as possible, the artist applied the paint straight from the tube to the board.

He used a little azo yellow medium, cadmium red, ultramarine and a generous amount of cerulean blue.

◄ **5** The overall colour of the wing at this point is a combination of cerulean blue and ultramarine, but there are hints of yellow, red and black (the primed board) showing through.

The artist modified the green in the left wing with areas of azo yellow medium. Then he went over parts of the back and top of wings with a mix of cerulean blue and ultramarine.

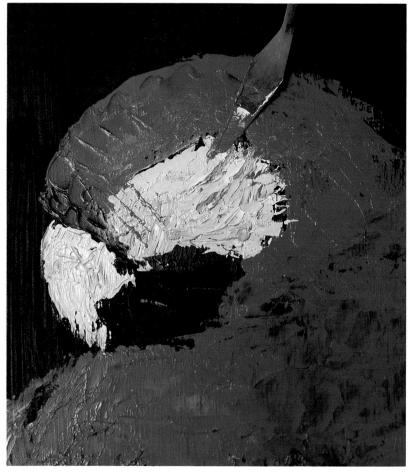

▲ **6** Using the small knife, paint the beak of the macaw with a mixture of yellow ochre and titanium white. For detailed work such as this, flex or bend the knife so that you use only the tip of the blade.

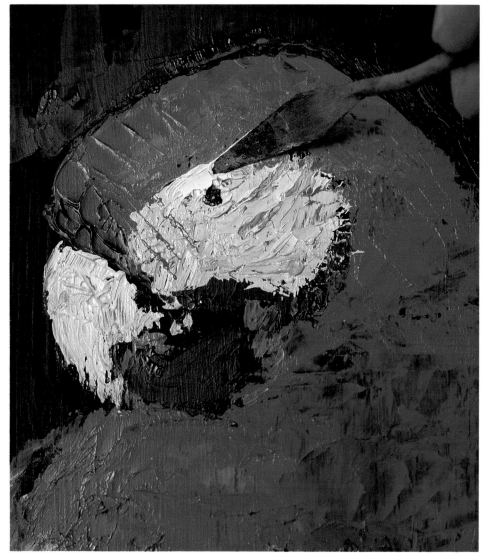

▲ **7** Add more white to the mixture you used for the beak, and paint in the face of the macaw. Touch in the dark lower part of the face with a mixture of ultramarine and burnt umber.

Then mix a little naphthol crimson and cadmium red, and with the edge of the knife, apply it in three short lines to the face. Then lightly drag the upper part of the knife across the right-hand edge of the face to add reddish tints.

At this point the artist felt that the head was too big, so he used his black mix to re-shape it and reduce its size.

◀ **8** For the iris of the eye (the coloured part) use a mixture of white and azo yellow medium, but notice that the paint isn't thoroughly mixed. The pupil is black. To help make the eye stand out, apply a white highlight above it, using the tip of the knife to create a broad stroke.

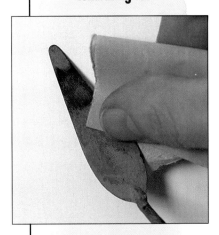
◀ **9** Highlight the outer edge of the beak with a thin white line to give it a round, three-dimensional look, again using the tip of the knife.

Now that the basic shapes and colours are mapped in, look for details to add.

◀ **10** For the white line on the tail feathers, make a long, sustained sweep with the edge of the large knife.

▶ **11** The artist felt that the wing was too big and too bright. Using the large knife, he re-shaped it and darkened it in places with the black mix.

Then he added cerulean blue straight from the tube to suggest rows of individual feathers.

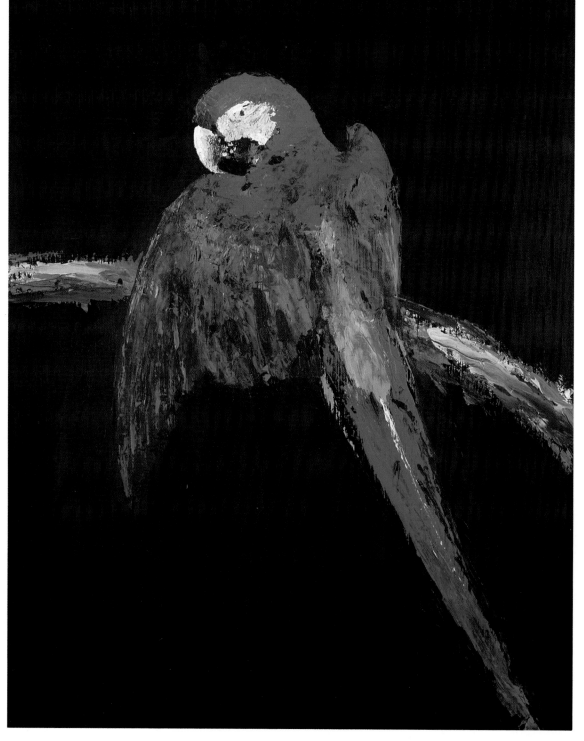

◀ **12** Put one dab each of yellow ochre, titanium white and burnt umber on the flat portion of the large knife. Then sweep it evenly over the board to form the branch that the macaw is sitting on. Use the tip of the small knife to scratch into the wet paint to add more detail and texture.

The finished knife-painting is full of energy with its many bright, exciting colours and angular knife marks.

Using liquid acrylics

Liquid acrylics are the most fluid form of acrylic paint. They handle much like inks, so you can use line and wash to capture the character of your subject with these deep, vibrant colours.

One manufacturer of liquid acrylics markets them as acrylic 'inks', hinting at their affinity with coloured inks. Both are similar to use, but liquid acrylics are coloured with pigments, while inks are dye-based, so the strong acrylic colours don't fade as much as inks (see Acrylic, Equipment 5).

You mix liquid acrylics with water to make washes, adding more paint for stronger colours, or extra water for delicate washes. Used on wet paper, you can create some beautiful flared effects very like wet-in-wet watercolour. Dry paint becomes waterfast, so you can overlap washes without the colours merging. Undiluted, some are opaque, allowing you to work light over dark.

Pen and brush work combine wonderfully. In this demonstration, our artist used bamboo pens with washes for a charming, illustrative effect. Bamboo pens are cheap to buy and lovely to use. Buy several sizes – fine, medium and thick – to allow for a range of marks, from thin, delicate flowing lines to thick, dark strokes. You can't avoid spills and blobs with these pens, but don't worry – these only add interest and spontaneity.

Liquid acrylics do justice to the colourful shop fronts in this Mayfair street scene, while the bamboo pens enabled the artist to pick out the architectural details.

▶2 Now complete the process on the right side, using both warm and cool greys. Outline the chairs and tables on the pavement, and the figures too. Use the warm grey for the closest figure (to bring it forward) and the cool grey for the figures in the distance (to make them recede).

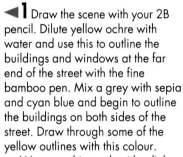

◀1 Draw the scene with your 2B pencil. Dilute yellow ochre with water and use this to outline the buildings and windows at the far end of the street with the fine bamboo pen. Mix a grey with sepia and cyan blue and begin to outline the buildings on both sides of the street. Draw through some of the yellow outlines with this colour.

Warm up this wash with a little sepia, then draw it in next to the existing grey lines to reinforce them. For the left foreground, switch to the medium bamboo pen.

▶3 Drop a little cyan blue on to the nib of the thinner pen (see Tip on page 91) and draw in the lamp post and sign to its left. Put in the paving stones with the cool grey. Blot off excess paint with blotting paper or tissue to stop the lines becoming too dark.

Using the No.10 brush, wet the sky with clean water. Load the brush with dilute cyan blue and wash it into the wet area so the paint spreads. Add more cyan blue to vary the wash in places.

Paint the distant buildings with the No.7 brush. Use yellow ochre for the light tones; mix in a touch of grey for the mid tones; add sepia to yellow ochre for the darkest tones. Allow the tones to blend together.

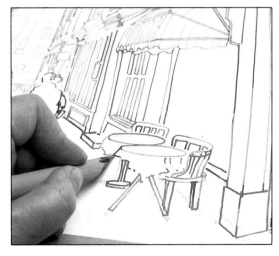

YOU WILL NEED

- A 12 x 17in sheet of 140lb Waterford HOT pressed paper, stretched on to a drawing board
- 2B pencil, palette
- Two bamboo pens: small and medium
- Jars of water
- Blotting paper, scrap paper and tissues
- Two soft round brushes: Nos.7 and 10
- An old toothbrush
- Eight Daler-Rowney FW Acrylic Artists' Inks: burnt umber, yellow ochre, raw sienna, sepia, process cyan, olive green, process magenta and black

►4 Mix a fresh grey with sepia and cyan blue. Use this for the dark buildings on the left side of the street. Add more cyan to vary the colour. Paint the brick wall at the corner of the street with sepia, adding some of your greys to vary the tone.

    Now touch in a few details. Apply burnt umber and yellow ochre to the sign beneath the brick wall; put in the shop signs and awnings towards the end of the street with varying mixes of burnt umber and magenta. Add a few dabs of this mix here and there to brighten up the area.

◄5 Make a series of very dilute washes for the paving stones – a grey with sepia and cyan blue, then yellow ochre, burnt umber and magenta. Wet the entire paved area and apply these washes to separate paving stones to give the impression of different coloured slabs. Leave some of the paving stones unpainted. These pale washes add subtle interest to the area. Use your sepia/cyan mix to wash over the rooftops, blotting them with tissue to soften the effect.

Tip

Blotting for texture
Keep a box of tissues close by when you work with liquid

acrylics. They come in very handy for blotting off excess paint. They can also be useful for introducing a bit of texture. Here, our artist blots the paint on the window pane with a piece of crumpled tissue to suggest its reflective surface.

►6 Increase the amount of sepia in your sepia/cyan mix for the buildings on the right side of the street, adding olive green as you work closer to the foreground for the lower areas on the shop fronts. Use sepia to depict the glass of the shop window (see Tip, left).

    When this dries, wash very pale cyan over the whole block of buildings on the right. Then bleed in some yellow ochre to vary the colours of the shop fronts slightly.

    Go back to the No.10 brush to paint the step and corner stone of the doorway in greenish-grey. Add burnt umber and a touch of magenta to make the rich colour of the door. Then put in the panel edging with yellow ochre to give the door a subtle, aged look.

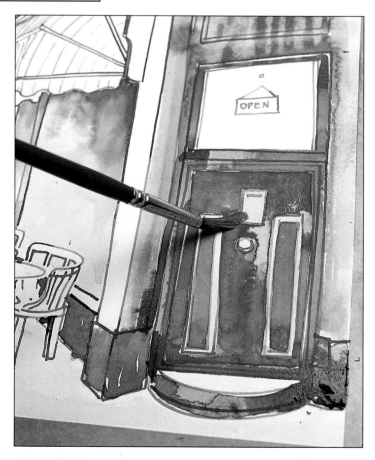

▶ 7 Stand back and take a look at your painting before putting in the details with the smaller No.7 brush.

Use various shades of olive green for the potted trees and the two signs on the left. Then paint the shop front next to the trees – add raw sienna to one of your grey mixes for the main part, applying dilute cyan for lighter areas and burnt umber for the darkest tones.

Use burnt umber to paint the chairs and table legs on the right and for the dark tones in the trees. Wash over part of the village shop sign with dilute cyan.

Put in the windows at the end of the street with mixes of sepia and cyan blue. Use a brownish-grey wash for the window in the door of the village shop, and black for some of the other windows.

▶ 8 Fill in the stripes of the village shop awning with a watery mix of magenta and a touch of yellow ochre. Strengthen the wash with more magenta for the darker stripes on the side. Paint the underside of the awning with a pale, yellowish grey.

Tip

Dropper caps
Many of the different brands of liquid acrylics have

droppers attached to the caps, similar to those on laboratory pipettes. These allow you to pick up small amounts of paint from the bottle and squeeze some out on to your palette. Use them to place a droplet of paint on to the bamboo pen, rather than dipping the nib into the bottle.

◀ 9 Put checks on the red tablecloths with dilute magenta and on the blue one with cyan. Add more cyan for the figure in the distance. Paint the coat of the central figure with sepia. Mix magenta and yellow ochre for the central figure's scarf and for the jacket of the closest figure, and fill in her shoes, skirt and bag with a strong black wash. Use yellow ochre for her hair.

Apply stronger washes to the buildings on the right (similar to the colours used for the shop in the foreground left). Then work around the picture with a strong grey and the bamboo pens, sharpening up details – the edges of the rooftops and window frames.

▶**10** Re-wet the paved area, and then, with a light grey mix, work on the shadows of the figures and the tables and chairs.

Add some texture to the paving stones by spattering on random colours from your palette with an old toothbrush. Mask out the areas you want to keep clean with pieces of torn scrap paper.

◀**11** Indicate the bricks on the side walls using burnt umber reddened with a touch of magenta and your medium-sized bamboo pen. Vary the colour by adding more burnt umber. Put in any finishing touches you feel are needed.

▼**12** The finished painting has all the illustrative qualities and bright colours associated with coloured ink drawings. The clear colours of the liquid acrylics have brought light and life to the picture, giving this colourful street a friendly, inviting atmosphere.

Creating texture in acrylics

There's a whole armoury of techniques for creating interesting textures with acrylics. Spattering, tonking and rolling paint are just a few of the most important ones.

Creating texture in your paintings may appear difficult, but all you need is a few basic techniques to help you produce a variety of textures which you can tailor to your subject matter.

Spattering This is a technique for applying paint in a field of erratic dots and blobs. Some of the most common objects you can spatter with are a comb, bristle brush, toothbrush and a decorators' brush.

Experiment with various brushes and some fairly watery paint mixes (on a separate sheet of paper, not your support) to see what effects you can produce. Spattering with a toothbrush, for example, can capture the fine texture, energy and feel of frothy waves at sea.

Tonking – named after the watercolourist Henry Tonks (1862-1937) – also allows you to create lively textures. You simply apply a wash, lay a sheet of paper over it, press the paper down with your hands then peel it off, leaving a highly textured surface. (You can tonk with acrylics, oils and even watercolours.)

Rolling You can apply paint with a small wallpaper roller, as our artist did in this demonstration. He rolled paint on to create irregular patches of broken colour which suited the markings of his moonlit cow.

Linear effects Use a phone card or an old credit card to make straight or curved lines, such as grass in our artist's demonstration.

▼ This happily grazing cow, spattered with greens, browns and white, blends peacefully into the background – at one with nature. See how many other textural effects you can see in this painting.

'Cow' by Peter Folkes, acrylic on paper, 15 x 22in

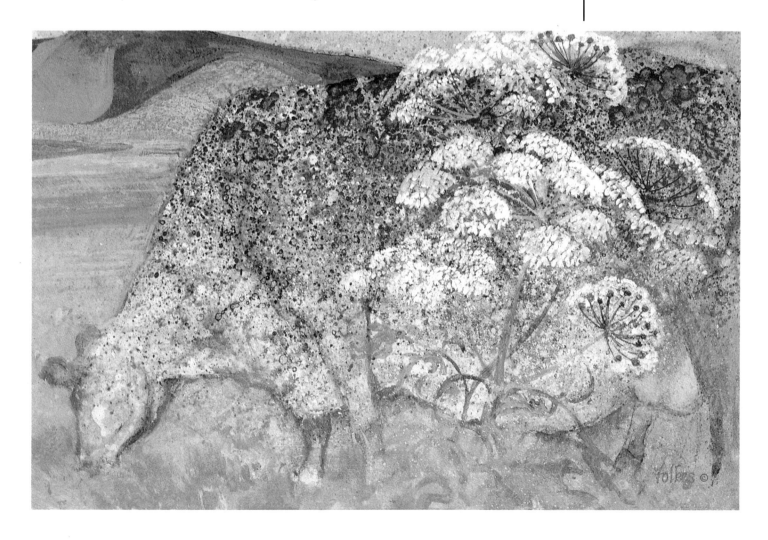

Trying out a variety of texture effects

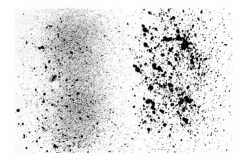  

Spattering Create fine dots of paint by loading a toothbrush with thinned paint then stroking the fibres with a palette knife. For larger spots of colour, load your bristle brush with thinned paint, then lightly tap the brush over the support.

Tonking (a) First apply a loose wash. While it's still wet, lay a sheet of newspaper over it, pressing down firmly. Then remove the paper – and see what you are left with. Blotting like this with newspaper lifts the colour and creates interesting textures.

Tonking (b) Try tonking with other materials such as cartridge/drawing paper or kitchen towel to produce different textures. You may even want to scrunch up the paper slightly and experiment to discover what suits your subject best.

Blotting and drying Spatter watery paint in two areas of the support with a soft brush. Blot one area immediately with newspaper (right), leaving irregular blobs.

Dry the other area with a hair dryer. Then wipe over the blobs with a damp cloth, removing the surplus paint and leaving white in the centre (left).

Rolling with acrylic paints A small wallpaper roller – or roller for lino printing – covered randomly with paint, creates interesting trails of broken colour. It's very important to vary the amount and thickness of the paint for maximum textural differences. For even more exciting effects, add texture paste.

Lines and curves You can add long straight or curved lines with the edge of a piece of cardboard, a phone card or an old credit card. Use these various linear marks to add interest and even texture to your paintings. Sometimes a piece of card will describe reeds or grasses more accurately than a brush.

Moonlight by the pool

▶ **The set-up** Cows – especially the mottled, brindled type – are one of our artist's favourite subjects. He has made numerous charcoal and pencil studies of them. Use these sketches as a reference, or better still, try your hand at sketching a few yourself.

Our artist worked first on the background then sketched in the cow. He continued with a variety of textures on the cow itself and then modified and developed the sky and field.

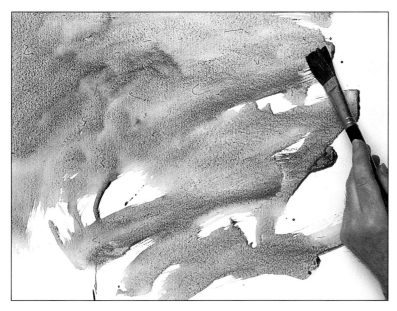

◀**1** First stretch your watercolour paper and, when it's dry, prime it with a thin coating of acrylic gesso. Then mix a fairly loose wash of burnt umber and ultramarine and apply it at random with your 1in wash brush.

(Keep the painting flat until you're ready to start drawing the cow – it's easier to tonk and to control the spattering.)

▲**2** Carefully lay a sheet of newspaper over the wet wash, and press your hand on it. Then peel it off. Repeat if you want a paler effect.

◀**3** Make a watery mix of yellow ochre, and spatter large blobs on to the textured ground with the 1in flat wash brush. Using a hair dryer, quickly dry the drops – but not thoroughly.

For this texture technique to work – both spattering and tonking – it's essential to gauge when the outer edges of the drops are dry while the centres are still wet. Wipe over the spatters with damp kitchen towel, removing the wet centres to create ragged, crater-like marks. Wipe again to get a cleaner look, if desired. Repeat with a little ultramarine and burnt umber.

A splash of masking fluid

The vivid colours of liquid acrylics can be combined with a bold use of masking fluid to create some lively images.

Masking fluid is usually associated with watercolour, but it's also compatible with liquid acrylics. Just as in watercolour, you can use it to protect the fine details of your painting while you apply the main washes. However, because liquid acrylics produce such vivid results, our artist decided to make use of the masking fluid in a more flamboyant fashion.

Firstly he applied it to the areas he wished to keep white – the turbulent water around his diver. Then he used it again, once the initial washes of colour had dried, to protect them from later washes.

When using masking fluid, you must think in terms of the negative – what you leave behind is just as important as the positive marks you make. If you want to leave areas white, you should mask them out at the start. This means you must think ahead.

With liquid acrylics don't use the colours too strong – that way you can keep your options open. Aim for a thin, watery mix – you can always strengthen the colour by washing over it again once the first wash has dried. Wash your hands thoroughly before you start – any fingermarks will show up under the thin washes.

Our artist chose a range of liquid acrylics – Golden Fluid Acrylics – with a consistency similar to Indian ink. They are intense colours made with lightfast pigments with good durability, flexibility and adhesion. But if you already have some liquid acrylics from another range, use them instead.

The set-up Our artist based this painting on one he'd done earlier. You can use his finished painting as a guide, or work from a sketch.

◀ **1** Loosely sketch the diver on the paper. Using the masking fluid and your old brush, mask out the water turbulence around the diver with vigorous strokes. Dab a few bubbles around the figure for a lively touch. Apply a thin line of masking fluid to define the back of the diver's head and her left arm. Leave this to dry.

◀ **2** Mix diarylide yellow with quinacridone red and add pyrrole red and water for a deep flesh colour. Try it on spare paper, then paint the face and chest with the No.4 round.

Mix pyrrole red and yellow to make orange and apply it to the thigh. Now use dilute quinacridone red to paint cheek, arms and body; overlay the chest and body with pyrrole red to indicate form – if you darken the areas of the body farthest away from you, the form becomes more three-dimensional.

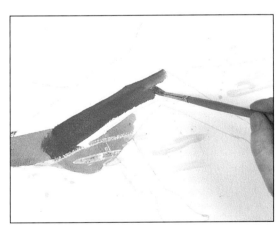

▶ **3** Paint the girl's hair with an almost black mix made from blue, diarylide yellow and quinacridone red. Don't paint the long streak of hair nearest the face – leaving it blank gives the diver more movement.

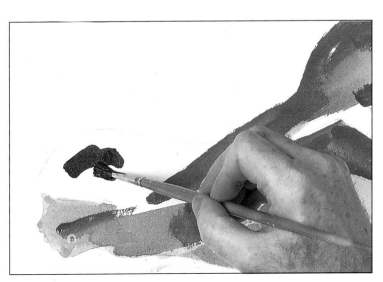

YOU WILL NEED

- [ ] *A 66 x 48cm sheet of 140lb NOT/cold pressed watercolour paper and a scrap of the same paper*
- [ ] *Masking fluid and an old No.4 or No.5 round hog brush*
- [ ] *Two brushes: a large wash and a No.4 round hog*
- [ ] *Palettes or two plastic egg boxes*
- [ ] *Large drawing board and gummed tape*
- [ ] *Water dropper*
- [ ] *Several jars of water*
- [ ] *Soft eraser*
- [ ] *Hair dryer*
- [ ] *Five Golden Fluid Acrylic colours (or equivalents): quinacridone red (crimson), pyrrole red (scarlet), phthalo green (emerald), phthalo blue, diarylide yellow (spectrum yellow)*

▶ **4** Now that the darkest colour is in, stand back and check the balance of tones in the painting. Assess which areas you wish to tone down when you add the turquoise wash in the next step.

Notice how the bold, vigorous brushstrokes indicate the speed of the diver. (It's also more fun to paint in this way, with lots of energy and enthusiasm.)

◀ **5** The next stage is to wash over the whole picture with turquoise for the sea. Protect any areas you don't wish to be tinted by the wash with more masking fluid. As before, apply it vigorously with your old brush. Don't cover the whole figure though – the areas of the diver farthest away from you would naturally be coloured by the depth of water, so leave these unprotected.

Leave the masking fluid to dry thoroughly – if it's not dry, the next wash will move it and drag it over the painting.

▶ **6** Mix phthalo blue and phthalo green with plenty of water. Test the mix on the spare paper – you want a rich turquoise. Use the dropper to adjust the water in the mix until you are happy with it. Now sweep the colour across the painting with your wash brush, starting just off the paper so the colour is smooth and even. Don't try to avoid the figure – just go straight over it.

If you get a build-up of paint on one edge, turn the paper upside down and repeat the strokes across the other way. Keep the paper fairly flat to prevent runs.

7 Leave the wash to dry. If it hasn't dried evenly or it isn't deep enough, reapply it, then leave it to dry again. When it is completely dry, rub off the masking fluid with your fingers or a soft eraser. Then feel over the page with your palms to pick up any bits you've missed.

Tip

Testing ground
Rather than experimenting on your painting, follow the advice of our artist and try out

each colour on scrap paper. You can even test successive layers of colour in this way, avoiding any unnecessary mistakes on your painting.

8 Now that the masking fluid has been removed, you can see exactly where our artist used it in step 5, before adding the turquoise wash. By masking only the areas of the diver nearest to him and the highlight on the far arm, he has given the figure plenty of form. Notice also how the sweep of masking fluid laid over the face has added to the sense of movement.

9 Our artist felt the face had lost definition, so he overlaid it with another flesh-coloured wash. He kept the effect lively by applying the paint unevenly, leaving some of the paler shade to shape the face.

▶ **10** The white lines defining the arm and shoulder looked a little harsh, so our artist washed over them with a wonderful splash of yellow. Since this is the complementary colour of the violet shades created by washing turquoise over the body, it makes the painting sing.

▼ **11** In the finished painting you can see how the vigorous brushstrokes and washes of colour combine to give the figure its sense of movement and form. It's like a freeze-frame shot of a diver, suspended in the moment of diving. Her position over to one side adds to the sense of movement, with the water in front alive with anticipation.

Optical mixing

The pointillist technique of optical mixing, originally done in oils, is perfect for fast-drying acrylics which almost eliminate the tedious time spent waiting for the little dots of pure colour to dry.

Pointillism is the technique of placing small, regular dots of pure, unmixed colour side by side on the canvas so that, when viewed from a distance, they react together optically, producing more vibrant colour effects than if the same colours were actually mixed together.

Georges Seurat (1859-1891) developed this technique towards the end of the nineteenth century. Using oil paints and working with pure colours – straight from the tube – he produced pictures which were composed entirely of dots of colour.

A drawback in this type of painting is the length of time oil paint takes to dry – the build-up is slow because you usually work wet over dry to retain the purity of the colours, so you have to work in stages, over a number of days. With quick-drying acrylic paints, of course, this problem simply disappears.

With this technique you can avoid the confusion of colour mixing, often a problem for the amateur painter, because you use paint straight from the tube. Although time-consuming, the pointillist technique is well worth the effort. The result is a shimmering picture exploding with fresh colours.

▼ **The shimmering quality of evening light captured here shows an attractive form of optical mixing in acrylics.**

Over a ground toned in raw umber (applied in vertical, striated, graded tones), the artist has applied dabs and dashes of colour so the ground shows between and, in places, gleams through the patches of colour. The complex broken paint surface gives the painting a wonderful luminosity.

'Winter Sunshine' by Michael B. Edwards, acrylic on board, 16 x 20in

Two old gardeners – and their dogs

◀ **The set-up** By taking many photographs for reference, artists can capture natural, unforced positions and movements for use later in their paintings. This artist takes many photos of people, and finds them extremely useful.

You need only one brush – a No.2 flat – for the entire painting, and you use colours straight from the tube, unless you are lightening them with titanium white. To create the dark colours, simply load a lot of one colour on top of another – the colours mix optically on the canvas.

◀**1** Before beginning to paint, spend some time making a good drawing from which to work. This gives you a chance to make adjustments and refinements – our artist changed the level of the feet for his painting.

Draw the figures on to the canvas board with the 2B pencil, using your reference drawing, and check that all proportions are correct. (Note the positions of the two little dogs – these change later on; there's no reason why you shouldn't alter and adapt as you see fit; the photo is only a starting point, not something to be copied slavishly.)

YOU WILL NEED

- ☐ *A 10 x 14in primed canvas board*
- ☐ *One No.2 flat synthetic brush*
- ☐ *2B pencil and an eraser*
- ☐ *Disposable palette*
- ☐ *Cotton rags*
- ☐ *Three jars of water*
- ☐ *Water atomizer (to keep paint moist on the palette)*
- ☐ *Nine Rembrandt acrylics: titanium white, lemon yellow, cadmium red, carmine, sap green, ultramarine, Rembrandt blue, raw sienna, burnt sienna*

▶**2** Start with the figure on the left. For his cap, make some initial dots in ultramarine, followed by similar marks in burnt sienna and raw sienna. Don't drag the brush in a conventional stroke – dab the brush on to the canvas and then remove it. Paint the hair using the same two colours and white.

Now apply colour for the face – first cadmium red, followed by lemon yellow, and finally burnt sienna mixed with titanium white.

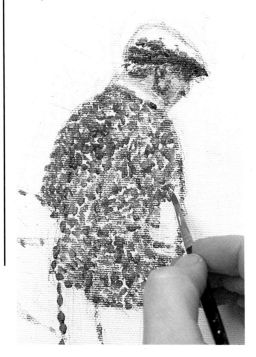

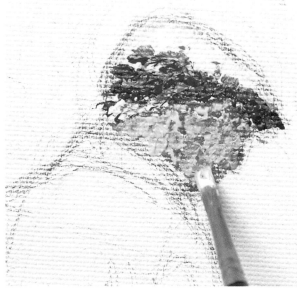

◀**3** Paint over the pencil outlines (both figures and dogs) with little dashes of ultramarine so you don't lose track. Then apply dabs of burnt sienna to the first man's jacket. All the colours show through when finished, and they mix in your eye to produce the right tones for fabrics, skin and so on.

▶ **4** Build up consecutive layers of ultramarine and burnt sienna to develop the volume of the jacket (add more dabs for the darker areas). Use raw sienna for the lighter tones and raw sienna with titanium white added for the highlights, such as on the shoulders and arm.

▼ **5** Still on the same figure, paint the shoes with the same two colours as the jacket, again making burnt sienna the predominant colour. Add white areas last for the highlight on the side of the shoe.

Tip

Take a break
Don't forget to distance yourself from your painting at regular intervals to check that the optical mixing works. And don't neglect the opportunity to take a break so that when you come back to your painting you can look at it afresh.

▼ **6** To finish this figure, use burnt sienna for the shadows on the trousers. Apply ultramarine over this for the mid-tones, then add some titanium white to the blue for the lightest highlights.

Use mixes of cadmium red and titanium white followed by yellow to dot in part of the background. Because of the speed at which acrylic dries, you can paint whole areas in one go – first the brick wall in the background, for instance, then the plants and bushes almost immediately afterwards.

◀ **7** Continue on the background with sap green – sometimes straight from the tube, sometimes mixed with white for a range of tones. Lay carmine over burnt sienna for the copper beech tree.

8 Apply dabs of cadmium red to the head of the man on the right. To develop the volume of his head, use sap green for the shadows and lemon yellow for the light tones, followed by burnt sienna mixed with titanium white. (Note the enhanced colour effect gained by using red, and its complementary, green, side by side.)

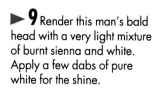

9 Render this man's bald head with a very light mixture of burnt sienna and white. Apply a few dabs of pure white for the shine.

10 Paint this man's shirt, using Rembrandt blue and titanium white. Apply burnt sienna to the darkest parts of his cardigan, then paint Rembrandt blue over the burnt sienna to form the folds and darks.

11 Use titanium white with a tiny amount of Rembrandt blue for the highlights – on the collar, the shoulders, the bottom back of the cardigan and his left elbow.

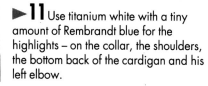

12 Establish the darkest folds in the trousers with burnt sienna. Over this apply pure raw sienna for the mid tones. To finish the trousers, mix raw sienna with titanium white for the highlights. (Note that the positions of the dogs are different – the artist has moved them so that they look into the picture, not out of it.)

▲**13** To strengthen the edge of the figure on the right, use a mixture of sap green and titanium white to push the background farther back. Make sure that all edges butt up to each other.

▲**14** Paint in the old garage doors on the right in ultramarine and sap green. Paint the post in raw sienna and burnt sienna with touches of red and blue for the darkest tones.

◀**15** Next paint in the little dogs. Use ultramarine, followed by raw sienna and burnt sienna for the dark areas. The tail of the dog on the right is mostly white.

▶**16** Paint the road with successive layers of ultramarine, raw sienna, carmine (mixed with white) and titanium white. The walking cane has two sides – a dark one (ultramarine and burnt sienna) and a light one (raw sienna with white). Now paint the grass in the foreground using sap green, blue lightened with white and lemon yellow in sequence.

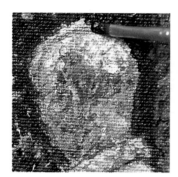

▲**17** Step back to examine the finished painting. The artist felt that she had painted the bald head too large, so she just extended the background colours to reshape the crown.

▶**18** After all that dabbing, the artist has created a vibrant painting, full of life. The colours shimmer and blend together in the eye. The only mixing of paint has been done with white. This was, in fact, crucial in the work of Georges Seurat, who felt that white increased the reflective powers of the other colours and evoked a feeling of natural light.

Interpreting what you see

Your subject may be as magnificent as the Taj Mahal, but it's how you interpret it that makes a good painting. Take liberties with reality to explore the potential of your subject and your imagination.

Edgar Degas (1834-1917) once said 'a painting needs as much fraudulence, trickery and deception as the perpetration of a crime'. Perhaps his criminal imagery was a little strong, but it does emphasize the idea that you can exaggerate and invent to make a good painting. Even from the most mundane of subjects, if you use your imagination and work with what's in front of you, you can create a fascinating picture.

This demonstration painting shows a view of London's Blackfriar's Bridge leading to some sky scrapers and St. Paul's Cathedral – a view that many artists have probably considered as a subject.

Our artist's painting, however, is unique. Instead of recording the scene exactly, he invents colours and textures to give it a magical and rather abstract quality. For example, he saw no reflections in the muddy water when he sketched and photographed the scene, yet in the painting they make up a large and interesting part of the composition.

The colours in the painting are most striking. Their bright, lively quality belongs very much with modern paints like acrylics. And they allowed our artist to create a personal, imaginative interpretation of his subject.

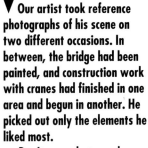

▼ Our artist took reference photographs of his scene on two different occasions. In between, the bridge had been painted, and construction work with cranes had finished in one area and begun in another. He picked out only the elements he liked most.
   Don't copy photographs. See them as a springboard, not a finishing point.

▼ You can see from these thumbnail sketches that already our artist brings in some imaginary reflections and plays around with their shapes and tonal values. He also uses these quick sketches to decide how high the waterline should go and where to crop the scene.

◄ Having decided on a composition, our artist made a small colour study to crystallize his ideas. He establishes his colour theme, the quality of light, the painting's atmosphere – and explores various textural possibilities.

YOU WILL NEED

- A 39 x 52cm sheet of white mount/mat board
- An HB pencil
- Our artist used a variety of brushes for this painting – you'll need at least four: a large mop, a medium mop, a 1in flat wash and a small round
- Trowel-shaped painting knife
- Jars of water and shallow tray for storing the brushes
- Palette
- Seven acrylic colours: French ultramarine, cadmium red, magenta, burnt umber, yellow ochre, phthalo green and titanium white

◀**1** With many of the decisions regarding composition already made, start by sketching the outlines of the main features with the HB pencil, paying special attention to the position of the horizon line. Our artist placed it high, on a third division, in fact, to give maximum emphasis to the enormous expanse of water.

Tilt the board at a slight angle and apply a loose wash of dilute French ultramarine all over the board with the 1in flat wash brush. Make the covering deliberately uneven to enliven the successive layers.

▶**2** Mix a wash of ultramarine warmed with a little cadmium red and, using the medium mop brush, fill in the sky, carefully cutting out the shapes of the buildings as you go.

Wait until this has dried thoroughly before continuing.

▶**3** Now apply a dilute wash of phthalo green over the water with the large mop brush, leaving the space for the foreground boat blank. Again, do this loosely, allowing the underlying blue to show through in places. This gives a sense of depth and translucency to the water.

These underwashes help to set the colour key of the painting and also establish a harmony which binds the painting together.

◄ 4 Paint some shadows on the buildings with your small round brush and a thin mauve mixed from cadmium red, ultramarine, magenta and plenty of water. Then start to indicate the reflections in the water with a mix of phthalo green, ultramarine and a tiny touch of cadmium red. Use your flat brush to make long, vertical strokes.

Tip

Brush care
If you don't wash your brushes immediately after use, leave them in water to prevent the

paint from drying on them and rendering them useless. If you leave them standing in a jar, the bristles resting at the bottom may bend and distort. Instead, lay them in a shallow tray of water, handles propped against the edge and bristles resting in the water.

► 5 Start to use thicker paint to build up the picture. Mix French ultramarine, cadmium red and titanium white and, keeping the paint quite dry, scumble loosely over areas of the sky with the small round brush. Let the underpainting show through in places to give the sky an airy quality.

◄ 6 Pick out the buildings to the right of St. Paul's with the painting knife. (The knife doesn't allow you to put in too much detail, so these buildings are kept firmly in the background. What you can achieve with the knife is sharp outlines that retain a fresh, spontaneous feel.)

Use the sky mix from step 5, darkened with burnt umber. Start at the outer edges of the buildings and slide the knife inwards, making block-like shapes. The paint doesn't settle in some areas – leave these gaps to stand as highlights.

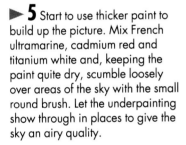

► 7 Add the buildings to the left of St. Paul's with a blue-grey mix, still using the knife. Then paint the cathedral itself with mauve-greys and a range of earthy yellows mixed from varying proportions of yellow ochre, white and cadmium red. Print the pillars beneath the dome – apply paint to the edge of your knife and press it down on the surface to make vertical lines.

Our artist wanted to reinvent the area around the cathedral by adding some foliage. Use phthalo green, with touches of yellow ochre and burnt umber for variation.

▶ **8** Mix a range of brooding greens for the clouds with varying amounts of phthalo green, ultramarine, yellow ochre, burnt umber, cadmium red and white. Obviously, clouds aren't normally green – this is an excellent example of colour used as an emotional element to express mood and convey a particular atmosphere.

Mix the paint thicker and drier now, and slide it lightly over the sky with the edge of the knife. This gives areas of broken colour through which you can see the underlying layers of paint.

Add some cranes in front of St. Paul's with a neutral blue-grey, printing them with the edge of the knife blade.

▲ **9** Knife painting encourages a broader handling of the paint so you don't become too involved in detail and labour the painting. Here, you can see the variety of lively and expressive marks our artist made with his painting knife.

Finishing the River Thames view

Our artist began this painting of St. Paul's Cathedral and Blackfriar's Bridge viewed from London's South Bank by covering the board with loose, dilute washes, then worked over these using thicker paint and blocking in the buildings with a painting knife.

▶ **10** Pick out the shape of the bridge with a pale green mixed from yellow ochre, white and a touch of ultramarine. Wait for this to dry, then paint the decorative red 'trimmings' with dilute cadmium red and the edge of the knife. Make your paint mixes thicker and brighter as you move towards the foreground to help the area advance.

◀ **11** Now paint the moored boats. Our artist used his photographs to help with details of shapes and colours, but avoided the temptation to put in too much detail. Observe the shapes carefully but paint them with brief lines and strokes, using neutral colours to keep them in their place in the background.

▶ **12** Start putting in the reflections in the water. Mix some stunning turquoises with phthalo green, and ultramarine, both mixed with varying amounts of white. Use stronger blue-green mixes for the darker reflections beneath the bridge and boats.

Apply the paint with sweeping downward strokes of the flat of the blade, using light pressure so the marks break up to suggest movement on the water's surface. (Don't overdo the reflections, or the water will look more like a patterned carpet!)

▶ **13** Continue painting reflections. Don't forget to relate them in shape and colour to the objects they reflect. St. Paul's, for instance, casts yellowish reflections – paint these with mixtures of yellow ochre and white, varied with either ultramarine or cadmium red. Paint the reflections of the skyscrapers with various mixtures of phthalo green and ultramarine. Use the edge of the knife blade to tick in a few red reflections beneath the bridge.

Tip

Knife edge
Painting with a knife produces some quite different results from painting with a brush. So if you want to add variety to your paintings, you can't beat a little knifework. Practice using the base, side and tip of the knife, and try out knives in different shapes – you can buy pear-shaped ones, long, straight ones or trowel-like ones.

▲ **14** Take a break – stand back and have a look at your painting from a distance. The reflections have been painted loosely with plenty of broken colour, giving them a wonderful, shimmering quality.

◀ **15** You may find it easier to evaluate your painting if you use a mount to 'frame' it. This cuts off the ragged edges and encloses it in a border so you can assess the balance of tones and colours within the image, and make any necessary adjustments.

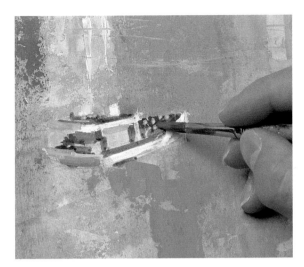

◀16a Paint the pleasure boat in the foreground using the small round brush. Begin with an underwash of pale blue, then pick out the shadows and highlights in various colours. Suggest figures on deck with tiny dots of paint, taking care not to make them look mechanical.

▲16b Continue adding detail to the boat, then put in a dark blue-green shadow beneath it, trailing behind into the boat's wake. Paint the vertical white radio transmitter with the side of the knife. Make its reflection less fine and regular than the transmitter itself. Stay with the knife to add the boat's frothy wake – ladle the paint on thickly and let it peter out away from the boat. For this, add plenty of white to the blue-green shadow colour.

▲16c This boat is one of the few areas of tight detail in the picture. Its foreground position attracts your attention and leads the eye into the picture. Notice how well the reflections work – the greeny-yellow one (towards bottom left beneath the boat) looks as though it's part of the reflection of St. Paul's which has been disturbed by the boat in its path.

Add white, horizontal lines for highlights with the side of the knife in areas of the water. Make the marks broken and textured to give the water a glassy appearance.

▶17 Loosely put in the barges by the bridge with the tip of the small round brush. Then indicate the cranes and gantries behind the bridge using cadmium red applied with the edge of the knife blade. Make any final adjustments you think necessary to the tones and colours.

►**18** Notice how our artist has built up the area around St. Paul's. The building itself is a focal point. Although there are trees, buildings and cranes around it, they are put in very loosely, blocked in broadly with the knife, so the main emphasis remains with St. Paul's.

However, this is put in loosely too – notice the pillars and windows beneath the dome. This keeps it in the background and gives its pale, dramatic silhouette great emphasis.

▼**19** Successive layers of transparent and opaque colour build up a lively, textured surface which plays a large part in the impact of the finished painting. The broken colour, which reveals small areas of underlying hues, sets up subtle and complex harmonies between the rather abstract shapes and colours – not only of the reflections, but in the skyline behind.

Because acrylic paint dries quickly, it is possible to develop successive layers of colour in rapid succession, without any fear of picking up and muddying the layers beneath.